THE COLOSSEU

CRITICAL INTRODUCTION
TO
DANA GIOIA

COLOSSEUM BOOKS
James Matthew Wilson, series editor

THE COLOSSEUM

CRITICAL INTRODUCTION
TO
DANA GIOIA

Matthew Brennan

Franciscan
University Press

Franciscan University Press
1235 University Boulevard
Steubenville, OH 43952
740-283-3771

Distributed by:
The Catholic University of America Press
c/o HFS
P.O. Box 50370
Baltimore, MD 21211
800-537-5487

Cataloging-in-Publication Data available from the Library of Congress

Cover Image: *Sunrise with Sea Monsters*. Oil on canvas by Joseph Mallord William Turner, ca. 1845. Granger Historical Picture Archive.
Printed in the United States of America.

Part of chapter IV, "The Poet as Critic and Public Intellectual," first appeared in the *South Carolina Review*.

Also by Matthew Brennan

POETRY:
Seeing in the Dark
The Music of Exile
American Scenes (chapbook)
The Sea-Crossing of Saint Brendan
The House with the Mansard Roof
The Light of Common Day (chapbook)
One Life

CRITICISM:
Wordsworth, Turner, and Romantic Landscape
The Gothic Psyche
The Poet's Holy Craft

In memory of Robert McPhillips
(1955-2019)

admired critic, much loved friend

CONTENTS

THE COLOSSEUM

CRITICAL INTRODUCTION
TO
DANA GIOIA

INTRODUCTION

Robert McPhillips has asserted that Dana Gioia is "the leading poet-critic of his generation" (*New* 33). Unquestionably, Gioia is a distinguished poet and critic. It is equally true that Gioia's reputation has often rested more on his work as critic, arts advocate, and public intellectual than as poet.

Gioia has often been more admired and deplored as a literary and cultural celebrity than as a poet, even though he has published five collections of poems; has served as the California State Poet Laureate; has won the American Book Award, the Poets' Prize twice, and the Aiken Taylor Award; and has been canonized in *The Norton Anthology of Poetry* and *The Oxford Book of American Poetry*. In the new century, his fame was spurred by becoming chairman of the National Endowment for the Arts (NEA) in 2003 and by receiving the Presidential Citizens Medal in 2008. Before Gioia stepped down from the NEA in 2009, his reanimation of the downtrodden agency brought him renown as newly launched programs such as The Big Read and Poetry Out Loud reached both communities across the map and arts lovers from all generations. Another important venture of the NEA under Gioia's direction, Operation Homecoming: Writing the Wartime Experience, staged workshops for soldiers, their families, and other veterans. The writings from the workshops composed the anthology *Operation Homecoming*, which the *Washington Post* listed among the best works of nonfiction for 2006. All this meaningful work came with a personal price, however: it kept Gioia from the writing desk, so much so that he began to wonder if the muse might desert him (Johnson 35). Earlier, in the nineties, he had drawn international attention as an iconoclastic critic for his controversial essay in the *Atlantic Monthly*, "Can Poetry Matter?" In the midst of the maelstrom surrounding the article, he published his second volume of verse, *The Gods of Winter* (1991). But while the hotly contested essay made Gioia something of a household name, it also overshadowed his poetry.

Even his initial emergence into the spotlight in the mid-eighties limited attention to his poems' intrinsic merits. While working as a marketing executive at General Foods and secretly publishing poems and criticism on the side, Gioia was unmasked in 1984 when his name made a list in *Esquire* of "Men and Women under Forty Who Are Changing America" ("Being Outted"). This accolade helped Gioia's first book, *Daily Horoscope* (1986), reach a wide audience of readers and critics; nevertheless, the irrelevant fame of his business career led some reviewers to caricature his volume as catering to an audience of yuppie commuters (Peters 50) or to equate it with "The Poetry of Money" (the title of Greg Kuzma's dismissive review). The book, of course, won much high praise for its virtues, but the penumbra of Gioia's day job made it easy to typecast. At the same time, as a prime example of the New Formalism (a term derisively coined by Ariel Dawson in "The Yuppie Poet"), Gioia's poetry elicited other reductive views that focused on his use of rhyme and meter. Notably, some wrongheaded critics simplistically considered the stylistic return to form as an act of political conservatism (Byers; Wakoski). His own defense of New Formalism helped the "movement" to reach its eventual place in the mainstream, but his success and fame as a critic further obscured his primary identity as "a poet who tries to do a good job" (qtd. in Lindner 6). Indeed, despite his prominent role as critical advocate of the movement, Gioia denies that he is "a formalist" poet himself because he writes a third of his poems in free verse and likes to invent his own forms.

These distracting controversies now seem of a different period. After his time at the NEA, Gioia resettled into the life of a poet. He began writing the poems that eventually made up *Pity the Beautiful*, *99 Poems*, and *The Ballad of Jesús Ortiz*, the old culture wars now a blur in his rearview mirror. Simultaneously, he has turned his critical attention toward the relations of Catholic writers with the American mainstream. As he approaches his seventieth birthday in 2020, he continues not only to write and publish individual poems for what will be his sixth volume of verse, but also to draft a long poem, "The Underworld," that figures to be a major work. In the last decade, then, Gioia has been able to cultivate his primary vocation, whose seedtime began in the rough-and-tumble working-class town of Hawthorne, California, where he discovered the joy of reading.

Chapter 1

LIFE AND CAREER

Hawthorne, California, the setting of Quentin Tarantino's films *Pulp Fiction* and *Jackie Brown*, is an industrial suburb of Los Angeles. After his birth in an LA hospital on December 24, 1950, Michael Dana Gioia grew up in Hawthorne with his two brothers, his sister, and his parents, Michael Gioia and Dorothy Ortiz Gioia. Together, the close-knit family shared an apartment in a triplex occupied by other relatives, with more kin residing in the adjacent building. His paternal grandparents and other elders had emigrated from Sicily and spoke an Italian dialect; his mother's side was Mexican. They were of the working class; his mother, a telephone operator, and his father, a cabbie and department-store salesman, often worked six days a week and opposite shifts. As a result, Gioia's childhood was lonely, but because the boy discovered early a love of books and art, his youth was "happy" (*Lonely* 2).

Gioia's mariner-uncle Ted Ortiz kept his vast collection of books, records, and musical scores in the apartment, where he stayed during leaves from the Merchant Marines. Though Gioia can't remember "ever seeing any adult relation, except [his] mother, read a book" (*Lonely* 3-4), his intellectual uncle's library in effect helped raise him. He may have preferred comic books, the fantasies of H. P. Lovecraft, and the Mars novels of Edgar Rice Burroughs that he would read to his own boys, but his earliest memory of reading involves paging through Uncle Ted's hardback copies of Thomas Mann and George Bernard Shaw. In the St. Joseph's Catholic School library, he found novels by Jonathan Swift and Daniel Defoe, and the public library was just three blocks from his home. By twelve years old, Gioia knew Edgar Allan Poe's "Annabel Lee" almost by memory, thanks to his mother's frequent heartfelt recitations of it ("The Hand" 33-34).

More precocious than his literary preferences was the boy's attraction to art and music, fostered by his uncle's reproductions of Renaissance paintings and *The Victor Book of Opera*. In fact, Gioia writes, "In fifth grade, I became passionately interested in art after seeing television specials on Leonardo da Vinci and Michelangelo. I haunted the enormous Hawthorne public library and over the next four years voraciously read through hundreds of art books." In a telling parallel that illustrates his weirdness, Gioia adds that he "studied European painting the way other boys immersed themselves in sports statistics," tracking "Old Master auction prices in a little notebook" (*Lonely* 8). He also became at twelve "a voracious gallery-goer":

> Satisfying my aesthetic appetites, however, depended on nagging my parents to travel from industrial Hawthorne to the widely scattered cultural shrines of Southern California. And so one Sunday my exhausted father drove across Los Angeles to smoggy San Marino so I might visit the Henry E. Huntington Library and Museum. I was keen to take in the late robber baron's Gainsboroughs, Reynolds, Constables, and Turners—the finest collection of Georgian painting outside London. ("Hand" 33)

The illustrations in the opera book inspired his own made-up plots. More important, in second grade he started piano lessons and later learned to play bass clarinet and tenor saxophone. Music ruled his passions during adolescence (Koss 154). His interests, however, combined pop culture and highbrow forms, science fiction and silent films, Igor Stravinsky and Brian Wilson. He took equal shares of glee from seeing on the street Moe Howard of the Three Stooges and violinist Jascha Heifetz ("Literary").

Another important element of his Latin environment and schooling by the Sisters of Providence was its Catholicism. Though in early adulthood he temporarily stopped attending Mass, his upbringing was saturated in the religion. Gioia remarks,

> Catholicism was everything to me. Growing up in a Latin community of Sicilians and Mexicans, one didn't feel the Roman Catholic Church as an abstraction. It was a living culture which permeated our lives. In parochial school, we attended Latin Mass every weekday morning, in addition to the obligatory Mass on Sunday; so for eight early years I went to Mass six days a week. The hymns we sang were still the classics of Medieval Latin liturgy. As altar boys, we learned all the ceremonial responses by heart. Our nuns scrupulously drilled us in liturgy, ritual, and dogma—which we tolerated—and recounted the flamboyant folklore of saints and martyrs—which we adored. (McPhillips, "Dana" 10)

In high school the curriculum Gioia studied encompassed Latin and theology as well as Augustine and Aquinas. If Catholicism pervaded his early life, it would gain an even greater significance to Gioia as he approached middle age.

In 1965, upon graduating from St. Joseph's grade school, he entered Junipero Serra High School, a Catholic institution run by the French Marianists. Here, besides his influential reading of Latin classics by Horace, Catullus, Virgil, and Ovid, Gioia edited the student newspaper, broke into print with his earliest reviews, and wrote "god-awful teenage poems" ("Literary"). Some of the articles betray his lifelong interest in pop culture, such as his first, a review of François Truffaut's film *Fahrenheit 451*, and his second, which evaluated an Isaac Asimov novel. But his elitist leanings crop up in a point-counterpoint column in which he answers negatively to the question "Is Pop Music Art?" The sixteen-year-old's next book review considered Andrew Field's biography of Vladimir Nabokov (Hagstrom and Morgan 115-16).

In 1969 he enrolled at Stanford University intending to major in music and become a composer, but after studying in Austria his sophomore year, he turned to English and discovered his calling as a poet. Twelve-tone music failed to engage him, and he strayed into the fields of poetry, which "fascinated" him. "Poetry chose me. I couldn't resist it," he has said (Koss 154). Back on campus, he published reviews in the *Stanford Daily*, and in 1972 he began contributing original and translated poems to *Sequoia*, for which he served as editor for two years. But his first published poem, "Words for Theodore," appeared in a joint Stanford–University of Southern California venture called *Stonecloud*. He studied William Wordsworth's *The Prelude* with scholar Herbert Lindenberger. Diane Middlebrook, the biographer of Anne Sexton, also taught him. Gioia learned German and French, won an English department honors competition with an essay on Poe's stories, and received a fellowship to graduate school in comparative literature at Harvard University.

Cambridge impressed on Gioia some formative experiences. Besides classes with Edward Said and Northrop Frye, Gioia profited greatly from courses with Elizabeth Bishop and Robert Fitzgerald, so much so that he devotes a chapter to each poet in his memoir, *Studying with Miss Bishop: Memoirs from a Young Writer's Life*. He took Bishop's course on modern poetry and became good friends with her, though in their social meetings their talk skirted the topic of poetry (McPhillips, "Dana" 14). Gioia took two courses from Fitzgerald, whom he calls "the single most important influence I had as a poet." Fitzgerald's History of English Versification required students to write lines of verse weekly in the meter currently being studied, exercises Gioia has described as "the most valuable learning I had as young poet," whose formal poems so far tended to be "halting and uncertain" (McPhillips, "Dana" 15). On his own he deepened what he knew about prosody by scanning Renaissance plays by William

Shakespeare, Christopher Marlowe, and John Webster. The verse of these plays taught him "how poetry is heard." The other formative experience at Harvard involved suffering. Not only was he lonely living in a squalid basement apartment on a dead end, but he also endured a mistreated back injury so painful he became suicidal. He "clung to poetry as a means of sanity" (McPhillips, "Dana" 13-14).

But after completing a master of arts in comparative literature in 1975, Gioia abandoned his goal to earn a doctorate and to spend his life in academia. He realized that he "was becoming a worse writer," his poems now striking him as "too studied and self-conscious. I was writing poems to be interpreted," he explained to Robert McPhillips, "rather than to register on the imagination and emotions" ("Dana" 20). For both literary and economic reasons, he left Harvard to return to Stanford, this time to earn a master of business administration. He kept writing poems—he left Harvard "to become a poet" ("Dana" 20)—but he stopped trying to publish verse; however, he did write reviews again for the campus paper and became poetry editor of Sequoia. From 1976 to 1980 he published only a handful of translations, parodies, and poems. At Stanford, he also took his only poetry writing seminar ever from Donald Davie; unfortunately, Davie's workshop proved "extraordinarily damaging" to Gioia as a still-developing poet because of Davie's rigid and limiting idea that American poets should follow the examples of either Yvor Winters or Ezra Pound ("Dana" 23). Nevertheless, outside of the class, seven of the students participated in a writing group that met weekly at members' homes or a bar. Sharing poems with John Gery, Vikram Seth, and Vicki Hearne proved helpful to Gioia and balanced the discouragement coming from Davie ("Dana" 24). Not until fall 1981 did he start submitting poems in earnest.

By this point, Gioia had met Mary Elizabeth Hiecke, a native of Los Angeles, and they married in 1980. In 1977, both finished their degrees and accepted positions with General Foods, in White Plains, New York. Marketing Jell-O and Kool-Aid for General Foods gave Gioia both a comfortable income and time during evenings and weekends to devote to writing. If he had rejected the creative writing workshop as the vehicle for his career, he never abandoned poetry. In fact, his path deliberately followed the model of the poet-businessman as embodied by T. S. Eliot and Wallace Stevens. In the preface to *Can Poetry Matter?*, Gioia explains that his critical essays betray various aspects of his identity—his being a poet, a reader of poetry, and "a critic working outside the academy" (xviii). The pieces on Eliot, Stevens, Ted Kooser, and the relations of business and poetry barely veil his struggles in the seventies and eighties to balance his occupation with his avocation. While moving up the corporate ladder, eventually attaining a vice presidency, Gioia kept his life as a poet secret from coworkers. In his essay "Being Outted" he says he went so far as to buy up all copies of the *New Yorker* on the company newsstand when his writings appeared in its pages. Gioia devoted fifteen years to this career, but his double life ended well before he abandoned business. Continuing like Wallace Stevens to write only during weekends and evenings, Gioia soon made waves with his poetry and criticism.

Daily Horoscope debuted in 1986 and elicited reviews in both newspapers and literary journals, most favorable, but some, such as those by Kuzma and Robert Peters, hatchet jobs. Simultaneously, the revival of meter, rhyme, and traditional form by such poets as Gioia, Brad Leithauser, Mary Jo Salter, Vikram Seth, and Timothy Steele was drawing fire from, among others, Ariel Dawson, Marjorie Perloff, and Diane Wakoski. This hostility functioned to bring the like-minded formalists together and spawned argumentative defenses through essays and special issues of journals such as *Crosscurrents* and *Verse*. Gioia's major contributions were "Notes on the New Formalism" and "The Poet in an Age of Prose," which were both reprinted in *Can Poetry Matter?* But the controversies sparked by these essays paled in comparison to the incendiary debates lit by the 1991 essay "Can Poetry Matter?" This contribution to the *Atlantic* made Gioia famous and led the next year to his similarly titled first collection of essays, a finalist for the National Book Critics Circle Award. In 1991 he also published his second book of poems, *The Gods of Winter*, which powerfully elegized the Gioias' firstborn, Michael Jasper, who died at four months old in December 1987 of sudden infant death syndrome. The births of the couple's other two children soon followed, Theodore Jasper in 1988 and Michael Frederick in 1993.

With the success of *Can Poetry Matter?*, Gioia decided in 1991 to quit the business world and to make his living as a poet and public intellectual. In late 1991, Gioia announced he was leaving his job as a vice president at General Foods. In a farewell memo he told his colleagues that he would now make a living by writing and teaching. Despite teaching for brief stints at such schools as Johns Hopkins and Colorado College and giving readings and lectures on college campuses, he has not depended on the academy for his livelihood —at least until he began teaching half time at the University of Southern California. Like Donald Hall, who left the University of Michigan in his forties for his native New Hampshire, where he became a freelance reviewer, textbook author, and poet, Gioia eventually left New York at age forty-five for his native California, where he has forged ahead as a professional man of letters—not a university specialist in creative writing. And, like Hall, Gioia has produced a wide range of works: criticism, textbooks, anthologies, translations, libretti, radio commentary, and of course poetry. In 1996, when he and Mary decided to move back to California, the family settled in Santa Rosa, Sonoma County.

After the death of Michael Jasper in 1987, Gioia recalls, he endured a long period of grieving in which he didn't write any poems for almost a year (Snyder 132). Though his crisis caused no loss of faith, it deadened him until after extended suffering he deepened his sense of compassion and "discovered," he explains, "that I had become a different person" (Koss 158-59). Moreover, he had become a poet who would try to write about the "difficult fundamental truths of human existence" (Snyder 132). The first consequence of this change was Gioia's masterful poem memorializing his lost son, "Planting a Sequoia."

Gioia's disenchantment with business played a part in his spiritual change as well. He stumbled upon Thomas Merton's *The Wisdom of the Desert* while browsing in a Manhattan bookstore and realized it released a hunger in his soul for "silence and solitude" (Koss 165). Merton helped him see that he needed "to reconnect more meaning-fully with my Catholicism," as Gioia puts it, and to undertake "the slow and difficult" pilgrimage toward redemption. He had to change his life (Koss 165, 174). As part of his evolution, on business trips for General Foods he carried Thomas à Kempis's *The Imitation of Christ* to help him "be a little less evil" (Koss 167).

Once he escaped from the business world, he gave lectures and poetry readings, continued to review books and music, contributed poems and essays to journals, delivered commentary on the BBC, and edited numerous textbooks and anthologies. In 1995, with Michael Peich he founded the influential West Chester Poetry Conference on Form and Narrative, and he also brought out a translation of the Roman tragedian Seneca. Later, he wrote a libretto for Alva Henderson's opera *Nosferatu* (published 2001). Finally, after a decade's wait, the same year that Graywolf Press brought out the libretto, it released his third collection of poetry, *Interrogations at Noon*. It won the 2002 American Book Award and solidified Gioia's stature. Gioia followed these books with two more collections of essays, *Barrier of a Common Language* (2003) and *Disappearing Ink* (2004). He also wrote a second libretto, for Paul Salerni's *Tony Caruso's Final Broadcast* (published 2005). It premiered in 2008 and was named the best new American chamber opera by the National Opera Association.

Despite this flurry of creativity, in the new century Gioia's literary pursuits took a back seat to a fresh endeavor: serving as chairman of the National Endowment for the Arts, a position he held from 2003 to 2009. For the next two years he directed arts and cultural programs for the Aspen Institute. In 2011, however, he became the first Judge Widney Professor of Poetry and Public

Culture at the University of Southern California. Until retiring in December 2019, he taught one half of the year in Los Angeles and wrote during the other half in Sonoma County. Freed by part-time teaching to reassume the life of a poet, Gioia brought out his fourth collection of poems, *Pity the Beautiful*, in 2012 and his fifth collection, a new and selected volume titled *99 Poems*, in 2016. This book won the 2018 Poets' Prize, and four years earlier—on the heels of *Pity*—he received the Aiken Taylor Award for Modern American Poetry. His next major work of nonfiction, *The Catholic Writer Today*, arrived in 2019, and *Studying with Miss Bishop: Memoirs from a Young Writer's Life* will follow in 2021. Working on the essays about Catholic writers had led Gioia to found yet another conference, the Catholic Imagination Conference, in 2015. In addition, in this decade, Gioia collaborated on two more operas: Lori Laitman's *The Three Feathers* (premiered 2014); and Salerni's *Haunted* (premiered 2019).

Deeply rooted again in his native California, from 2015 through 2018, Gioia served the state as its poet laureate, perhaps the role that has fit the poet–public intellectual best. In his mission as laureate he hosted community poetry readings in all fifty-eight counties. When not traveling, Gioia has worked to strengthen the ecosystem of his California home, protecting native species and restoring his twenty acres of oaks and redwoods to their natural state. Gioia the poet-steward likes his California hills "the way God landscaped" them (Koss 176). In October 2019, however, just two months before his retirement from teaching, the Kincade Fire reduced his neighbors' homes to ashes and roared through the Gioias' well-trimmed property. Miraculously, it failed to ignite their house, though their dwelling and two outbuildings suffered some smoke and ash damage. Gioia's ongoing care to restore the earth had saved their home and many trees.

Chapter 2

POETICS

One guide to Dana Gioia's aesthetics lies in his allegiance to the New Formalism. Less an organized movement than a generational change in poetic sensibility, it drew together poets dissatisfied with the entrenched tradition of the first-person lyric in free verse and what Gioia has called "the bankrupt theory of the perpetual avant-garde" ("Symposium" 90). In *The New Formalism: A Critical Introduction*, Robert McPhillips sums up the sensibility, sometimes called "Expansive Poetry," as "a new aesthetic that combined traditional forms and genres," including narrative, "with contemporary language and subject matter" (6). What helped foster the movement, McPhillips notes, was the controversy that Diane Wakoski sparked in an unmeasured blast of unnamed poets and a still-unnamed development in American poetry (*New* 4). In a 1986 article in *American Book Review*, Wakoski, a staunch practitioner of free verse, lambastes the "new kind of 'il-literati'" who espouse "tradition" and "preach metrics in old-fashioned ways, often simply being interested in 'form,' whatever that is, for the sake of form" (3). McPhillips emphasizes that Wakoski "actually believes those who use traditional forms could only be supporters of Reagan's conservative agenda." The positive result of Wakoski's zealotry, as McPhillips puts it, was that it led isolated but like-minded poets "to see themselves as part of the loose movement that would be identified as the New Formalism" (*New* 4-5).

Pivotal in helping this loose movement cohere was Gioia's polemical essay "Notes on the New Formalism," which originally appeared in the *Hudson Review* in 1987. In this essay, Gioia defined the unique situation formalist poets found themselves in as the eighties closed: "The New Formalists put free-verse poets in the ironic and unprepared position of being the status quo. Free verse, the creation of an older literary revolution, is now the long-established, ruling orthodoxy, formal poetry the unexpected challenge" (29). He then defends the artistic uses of meter and advocates treating both democratic and high-cultural subjects. Here Gioia also underscores how the revival of narrative and form can expand the appeal of poetry to audiences bored by "the short, autobiographical, free-verse lyric" (37). In laying out a set of literary principles in the special issue of *Crosscurrents*, Gioia emphasizes that the typical expansive poem is not confessional. In describing the "movement," Gioia notes its members' common dismissal of "self-indulgent autobiography," especially the brand fostered by the Beats and Confessional poets ("Symposium" 89-90).

But Gioia's poetics is more complex than the manifestos of the movement might suggest. For one thing, while Gioia has avoided "self-indulgent autobiography," he has not rejected using personal experience as poetic fodder, even if his first-person speakers are often personae. The many elegies to his firstborn son clearly come from his life, and love poems such as "Parts of Summer Weather," "Summer Storm," and "My Dead Lover," as well as lighter poems such as "Cruising with the Beach Boys," all seem to build, in part, from memories, no matter how they may be altered. "Special Treatments Ward" is harrowingly personal. For another thing, Gioia differs from most of the New Formalists in his employment of form and meter. Most striking, he uses free verse in one-third of his poems. Unlike a rigorously metrical poet such as Timothy Steele, Gioia likes to mix formal and free verse, and occasionally, as in "Summer Storm" and "Words," he shapes his lines by accentual meter. Furthermore, Gioia writes a looser verse than Steele; in his method, Gioia more closely follows Frost. As Kevin Walzer observes in *The Ghost of Tradition*, "some of his most distinctive poems (such as 'Lives of the

Great Composers' from *Daily Horoscope*) are formal experiments of his own devising, based on neither a metrical form nor free verse, but on forms of music" (41). "The Litany" in *Interrogations at Noon* is a later example of metrical innovation. Altogether, the first two books contain few poems in fixed forms—a sestina, a double triolet, two ballads, and one unrhymed sonnet. Clearly, Gioia has no interest in making rhyme and meter the rule in poetry; they are merely techniques that can lead to "compression and expressivity" (Koss 156). Unlike other New Formalists, he never saw New Formalism as a break from modernism. "Why throw away the greatest period of American poetry?" he asks (Johnson 27).

This last point raises the greatest difference between Gioia and some of the New Formalists: their relation to modernism. "In the Poet in an Age of Prose" he complains about the "parochialism" of some "formalists who are essentially anti-Modernists" and who "are more likely to imitate than innovate" (230). The modernists have shaped his poetics more strongly than other writers, including his attempt to use personae. As an undergraduate he carried Pound's *ABC of Reading* with him everywhere, began reading Pound's poems, and wrote reviews of Pound, Eliot, and Montale for the *Stanford Daily* (McPhillips, "Dana" 12, 10). Indeed, Gioia divides his work into two branches: one in the tradition of Hardy, Auden, and Larkin, and one in the tradition of European modernism. The latter influence shows in poems such as "My Secret Life," "An Elegy for Vladimir de Pachmann," and "Elegy with Surrealist Proverbs as Refrain," not to mention his translations of Montale and Rilke (McPhillips, "Dana" 16, 24). In addition, Gioia has written admiring essays on Wallace Stevens, T. S. Eliot, Robert Frost, and Robinson Jeffers, and has always believed that "*all* art" must "be innovative." Thus, Gioia states, "the enduring challenge of Modernism is to make poetic form dynamic, to insist it become a mode of discovery" ("Symposium" 89). Although "Modernism is dead," Gioia believes that writers "must find a way to reconcile the achievements of Modernism with the necessity of creating a more inclusive and accessible kind of poetry"

(McPhillips, "Dana" 16-17). Consequently, rather than use traditional forms, Gioia prefers to experiment "with new forms or" to play "with the rules of traditional patterns to achieve something slightly unexpected." This approach enables him to surprise both himself and readers ("Symposium" 88). For example, even the recent uncollected poem "Words, Words, Words" surprises with a novel five-line stanza: it rhymes *abaca*, and while employing iambic pentameter in four of the lines, Gioia shortens the penultimate line to iambic dimeter.

Gioia's chief concern, then, is for stylistic diversity, which he finds in the poets he admires most, such as Weldon Kees and Elizabeth Bishop. Tellingly, Gioia has called W. H. Auden his "favorite modern poet," noting that Auden excels at "formal and musical variety" (Snyder 126, 139). Donald Justice is another model, whose stylistic diversity and use of modernism are the subjects of the essay "Tradition and an Individual Talent." To Gioia, as he explains in "Notes on the New Formalism," free verse and meter are "complementary techniques," modes of the English language equally viable to serious poets (41). Other midcentury modernist models emerge in Theresa Malphrus Welford's thorough study of links between the British Movement poets and the American New Formalist poets. Welford reports that when Gioia took the poetry writing class from Donald Davie at Stanford, he considered him a kind of mentor (81), even though his influence was damaging. Furthermore, according to Welford, Gioia has revealed that while he finds poems by Davie, Thom Gunn, and Elizabeth Jennings admirable, Philip Larkin is both one of his "poetic heroes" and a significant influence (88).

Equally important to Gioia's poetics as form and stylistic diversity is his Catholic faith. Though his poems' subjects are rarely religious —with exceptions such as "Prayer," "Prayer at Winter Solstice," "Pentecost," "The Litany," and "The Angel with the Broken Wing" —Gioia insists that his verse is theological (Snyder 136). He told Erika Koss, "I am a Catholic, and I am a writer"; one can't "separate the two identities" (169). He explains what most makes his poetry

Catholic: "the redemptive role of suffering" and "the sacramental use of symbols" (Koss 173). Gioia locates the theme of suffering and redemption in the narratives of his first two books and calls them exemplars of "the Christian mythos, especially the journey from despair to grace" (Snyder 136). His use of sacramental symbols, he remarks, depends on his building poems "from the daily particulars of real life" (Koss 173). These particulars—not only a poem's images but also its experiential sounds and rhythms that readers respond to physically—embody or incarnate truths. For Gioia, poetry communicates best not through abstractions but through the intellect, the feelings, and the senses all at once (Koss 164). Above all, the Catholic writer must aim, as all serious writers do, "to create powerful, expressive, memorable works of art." Gioia insists, "The Catholic writer must," like any other, "master the craft in strictly secular terms" ("Catholic Writer" 41).

Whereas his aesthetics of form and artful expression connects him to a tradition of poets including Auden, Bishop, and Larkin, the current culture lacks a poetic tradition of Catholic writers. So Gioia stands alone, looking into the past for models—Dante, Shakespeare, Baudelaire (Koss 170). In *The Catholic Writer Today*, however, he does write approvingly of several Catholic poets, including Gerard Manley Hopkins, John Donne, and Dunstan Thompson. In particular, Elizabeth Jennings would seem a likely model for a Catholic New Formalist. She "returned the Catholic perspective to the mainstream of British verse" in well-crafted lyrics ("Clarify" 120). Gioia's admiration for Jennings underscores perhaps the foundational belief of Gioia's poetics: that the lyric "is both sacramental and metaphysical," for it both displays "the surface" of reality and hints at "what lies beyond the physical senses" (Snyder 127). Surely Hopkins, who perceives "God's Grandeur" in "skies" and "finches' wings," reveals that the divine "is everywhere if you know how to look," but so too does Jennings (Koss 173).

Ultimately, as Gioia has written, theory matters little compared to actual poems. In describing his process of writing poems in an interview with Michelle Johnson, Gioia sounds notes that echo statements by the Romantics on how poems get made. He relies on "intuition" and so is most pleased when a gestating poem surprises him. He adds, "the poem is invisible until you write it down"; at the start, you have "only impulse and intuition." As a result, he depends on the physical sound and rhythm of a poem to establish enchantment "before it communicates" (28, 30). As he says in *Poetry as Enchantment*, "All poetic technique exists to enchant—to create a mild trance state in the listener or reader." Thus the start of a poem is primal. He told Robert Lance Snyder, "for me, inspiration has always been involuntary—sudden, surprising, and often disturbing." The poem for Gioia starts "as a small epiphany" when "some ordinary object or event makes a small rip in the fabric of time and place," causing him to "sense something lying beyond" (131-32). For this reason Gioia begins composition like Wordsworth, by saying lines aloud before he commits anything to paper (Johnson 34). Gioia says, "The finished poem attempts to recreate that experience of awe and wonder"—the small epiphany—with which the poem began (Snyder 132). Gioia is "a very slow and self-critical poet," however, which suggests, like Alexander Pope, that he views the poet as a maker (Johnson 35). As he told Robert McPhillips, "I normally work on poems for years before publishing them" ("Dana" 27). What he tries to make is a poem that creates "a sort of dance between the text and subtext," a dance that releases "the reader's intuition and imagination." Finally, for Gioia, his poetics boils down to wanting to do a good job, making poems that readers will find "musical, moving, and memorable" (Johnson 28). These readers are not only "the literati," but also "any alert and intelligent reader" (Snyder 132-33).

Chapter 3

POETRY

DAILY HOROSCOPE (1986)

Dana Gioia's debut volume displays many of the characteristics promoted as New Formalist, but it diverges sharply from them as well. In several poems, Gioia purposely avoids a first-person point of view. A few poems use first-person plural ("we"), including "Song from a Courtyard Window" and the humorous "Thanks for Remembering Us"; another group uses a second-person perspective, among them the six-section sequence of part II, "Daily Horoscope." Some of the strongest poems center on a character—"An Elegy for Vladimir de Pachmann" and "Bix Beiderbecke"—while in "Speech from a Novella," "Four Speeches for Pygmalion," "In Chandler Country," and "The Room Upstairs," Gioia experiments with the dramatic monologue, another way to skirt the personal. By developing narratives, these poems further typify the so-called expansive poem.

Daily Horoscope contains many poems in meter and rhyme. "The Man in the Open Doorway," "Parts of Summer Weather," and "The Sunday News" are deftly written in rhymed quatrains, with some differences in meter; "Cruising with the Beach Boys" is written in iambic pentameter with irregular rhyme; and "An Emigré in Autumn" is inventively shaped into a pair of ten-line stanzas in long meter (four accents per line) that rhyme in only the seventh and last lines. In addition, blank verse undergirds multiple poems, for instance, the monologues "The Room Upstairs" and "In Chandler Country." Finally, "The Country Wife" exemplifies a double triolet, and "Sunday Night in Santa Rosa" is an unrhymed sonnet. Gioia omits the sonnet from his selected poems, *99 Poems*, but the sonnet demonstrates metrical variety:

> The carnival is over. The high tents,
> the palaces of light, are folded flat
> and trucked away. A three-time loser yanks
> the Wheel of Fortune off the wall. Mice
> pick through the garbage by the popcorn stand.
> A drunken giant falls asleep beside
> the juggler, and the Dog-Faced Boy sneaks off
> to join the Serpent Lady for the night.
> Wind sweeps ticket stubs along the walk.
> The Dead Man loads his coffin on a truck.
> Off in a trailer by the parking lot
> the radio predicts tomorrow's weather
> while a clown stares in a dressing mirror,
> takes out a box, and peels away his face. (87)

Only four lines scan as regular iambic pentameter—2, 6, 8, and 12. The other eight all seem to manifest singular sequences of rhythm and metrical substitution. For instance, lines 9 and 13 both begin with headless iambs (*Wind / while*) but unfold differently: the second foot in line 9 forms an iamb with the verb demoted in pronunciation (sweeps *ticket*) before returning to iambics, whereas line 13 follows its headless iamb with an iamb (a *clown*) but then introduces a trochee (*stares in*). In these final two lines, Gioia evokes empathy for the man who wears the mask of the clown and who, in removing it, restores his humanity and his true self. So, in its handling of blank verse, "Sunday Night in Santa Rosa" meets Gioia's goal of stylistic variety.

Besides using form, *Daily Horoscope* anticipates the call of expansive poetry to find subjects from popular culture as it treats jazz, the noir detective novel, the carnival, and rock music. A prime example is the third poem in the book, "Cruising with the Beach Boys," which treats pop culture in meter and rhyme. Here are the first two of four stanzas:

> So strange to hear that song again tonight
> Traveling on business in a rented car
> Miles from anywhere I've been before.
> And now a tune I haven't heard for years
> Probably not since it last left the charts
> Back in L.A. in 1969.
> I can't believe I know the words by heart
> And can't think of a girl to blame them on.
>
> Every lovesick summer has its song,
> And this one I pretended to despise,
> But if I was alone when it came on,
> I turned it up full-blast to sing along—
> A primal scream in croaky baritone,
> The notes all flat, the lyrics mostly slurred.
> No wonder I spent so much time alone
> Making the rounds in Dad's old Thunderbird. (5)

The nostalgia for the adolescent past allows feelings that the speaker thinks he has outgrown to rejoin his adult consciousness; the pop images that trigger them seem straight out of George Lucas's *American Graffiti*—except that, by the poem's end, the remembrance of unrequited desire brings the speaker to the brink of tears. Gioia barely escapes sentimentality through his unobtrusive but surehanded form. The eight-line stanzas comprise lines in iambic pentameter that mostly rhyme but are sometimes slant and in a few cases rhyme not at all. With the conversational syntax, these variations in rhyme lend the poem spontaneity. As McPhillips says, Gioia "makes his unabashed self-pity moving, to a large extent because his use of meter and rhyme provides just enough formality to objectify the speaker's emotions" (*New* 39). Coming after poems invoking the Bible

("Jacob's Ladder") and depicting an easterner's snobbish reaction to western topography ("California Hills in August"), "Cruising with the Beach Boys" surprises readers with its irresistible pop-culture appeal, much like the rock song interrupting the speaker's night drive. "Gioia's poem explores not only how the teenager is 'father to the man,'" James Matthew Wilson observes, "but how American mass culture creeps through the cracks of even the most cultivated personality" (*Fortunes* 94).

If "Cruising" exemplifies aims of Expansive poetry, Gioia nevertheless carves his own path in his collection's diversity of not only forms and subjects but also objective and personal points of view. Besides pop culture, for example, there are poems that explore high culture: the paintings of Hieronymus Bosch and Fra Angelico; the music of J. S. Bach, Niccolò Paganini, and Robert Schumann; histories of tobacco and Victorian pornography; and the myth of Pygmalion. And besides the many poems founded on an objective point of view, many poems, especially in the book's last part, adopt first-person perspectives, and often in free verse. Two lyrics from part V, "The End of a Season" and "View from the Second Story," both use "I" and unfold situations that are personal, but they are perhaps too general to be labeled autobiographical. Furthermore, in both poems, Gioia tightly controls his free verse. "The End of a Season" presents sensuous images and gains artistic control of directly expressed emotion through its stanzaic structure. The poem opens with two six-line groups that start sequentially with "I wanted to tell you" and "I wanted to wake you":

> I wanted to tell you how I walked tonight
> down the hillside to the lake
> after the storm had blown away
> and say how everything suddenly seemed so clear
> against the sparkling, rain-soaked streets
> cold and bright as starlight.

I wanted to wake you up, despite the hour,
and drag you out into the dark
crisp air to feel the end of winter,
the cold we cursed so long
slipping away—and suddenly so precious
now that it was leaving. (76)

These symmetrical stanzas then veer into a quatrain that throws off the poem's balance and embodies the speaker's unease: "But there is no one to come back to now, / only the night" (76).

"View from the Second Story," unlike most of Gioia's free-verse poems that divide into stanzas, is a single, nineteen-line cluster, but it cleanly joins immediate experience, the weather, and the coming darkness:

There were no colors in the sunset.
Rain had been coming down for hours,
and the winter sky was a bright grey
against the windowpanes. Lights were coming on
in all the other houses, but here
only weak sunlight from the rain-streaked glass
dissolving in the shadows of the furniture.
How easily the room comes back again.
I can still feel the cold, still hear the cars
streaking down the rainy avenues below us.
You are in the bedroom, sleeping, or crying.
I don't know which. Am I afraid to look?
And I am still standing at the wide window
looking for something beyond the dark rows
of winter trees and houses, feeling the cold air
that somehow finds its way between the cracks
of any windowsill, and I am waiting,
listening to the rain while the air which seemed
invisible turns gradually to black. (75)

In lines that scan loosely as iambic, Gioia evokes the memory of a night when his speaker's environment turned ominously dark and not only corresponded to the current climate of rainy cold and encroaching darkness, but also symbolized the aftereffects of an unspecified domestic disturbance. While "You are in the bedroom, sleeping, or crying," the alienated speaker—who "still" can feel "the cold" of the rainy winter day—is afraid but expects what comes next as night arrives; thus, as the poem ends, he is "still standing at the wide window / looking for something beyond," while "the air" ominously grows "black" (75). The poem expresses strong feeling directly, but it is personal rather than confessional. Gioia's depiction of the weather forms an objective correlative for a vivid but ambiguous emotional mood that the first-person speaker, like the reader, only partially comprehends.

Like its well-crafted individual poems, the structure of *Daily Horoscope* itself helps delineate its themes. This debut volume, like all of Gioia's first four books, is coherently organized into five parts. The opening part contrasts the West and the East, California and suburban New York, "In Chandler Country" and "In Cheever Country." It also treats the world of business and work in several guises: air travel in "Waiting in the Airport" and "Flying over Clouds"; commuting and parking lots in "Eastern Standard Time" and "In Cheever Country"; and businessmen after work in the empty office or at a diner ("The Man in the Open Doorway," "Men after Work"). Part II comprises the title sequence, and part III presents poems that center on characters or function as monologues. Part IV treats poems of travel, and the book closes in part V with works on love and memory, combining several personal poems, such as "Photograph of My Mother as a Young Girl," with the narrative "The Room Upstairs."

The two opening parts have elicited the most praise and the most controversy. Based on these first poems, Kuzma reduces the book to "the poetry of money because what it values most are material things" (114). But to read these poems as Kuzma does is to read them

superficially. More accurately, the poems explore the conflict between our practical, routine lives and our desire for an idealized but
ultimately impossible transcendence, the desire to see beyond the
material surface of reality and, as Wordsworth would say, to "see into
the life of things." It is a universal theme that Wordsworth plumbed
in the sonnet "The World Is Too Much with Us," where our constant
"getting and spending" keeps us from seeing with vision. McPhillips
labels this theme "visionary realism." He explains, "Gioia's poems are
marked by a distinctive poetic style of visionary realism in which
memory imbues details of the ordinary world with a sensuous lumi-
nosity, making them at once seemingly tangible yet tantalizingly
elusive, as if existing in a border region between time and eternity"
(*New* 36). Visionary realism, then, approximates what Gioia describes
as "the interpenetration of the sacred and the mundane" (Koss 173).

McPhillips perceptively explicates how Gioia pursues visionary
realism in the title sequence—part II of the book—noting how
daily life, despite its costs to individual desires, offers brief moments
when "you press against / the surface of impenetrable things":

One

more summer gone,
and one way or another you survive,
dull or regretful, never learning that
nothing is hidden in the obvious
changes of the world, that even the dim
reflection of the sun on tall, dry grass
is more than you will ever understand.

And only briefly then
you touch, you see, you press against
the surface of impenetrable things. (27)

Because this sequence of poems explores when "another world / reveals itself behind the ordinary" (29), the language is often general,

unlike the concrete diction limning the views through the window of a commuter train in "In Cheever Country." In fact, one reviewer complained that when Gioia evokes the "rarified" realm that is "out of reach," the writing becomes "abstract" and "keeps experience at a distance" (Flamm 45). In part, Matthew Flamm may well be reacting to Gioia's use of general statements in his poems. Most contemporary poets rely on the image alone to convey meaning, finding "no ideas but in things," and thus they avoid declarative utterances. In contrast, Gioia often incorporates general statements. Consider the following examples: "Nothing is so small / that it does not return" ("Daily Horoscope"); "Gravity / always greater than desire" ("The Burning Ladder"); "vagrant sorrow cannot bless the dead" ("Special Treatments Ward"); "To name is to know and remember" ("Words); "To learn that what we will not grasp is lost" ("The Apple Orchard"); "What we conceal / Is always more than what we dare confide" ("Unsaid"). But McPhillips astutely reads "Daily Horoscope" alongside the more explicit, image-rich commuter poem, and he finds that "despite the absence of a first-person speaker," the title poem "is no less than a spiritual autobiography of the poet," who at the time still worked in corporate America and lived in Westchester County (*New* 43).

Although Kuzma reads "In Cheever Country" thematically as a warning that we should "protect our investments" (118), the poem is actually a powerful demonstration of what the Romanticist J. Robert Barth, SJ, calls the "sacramental imagination," a rough synonym of "visionary realism" that involves perception of the spiritual through the material; for Barth, both sacraments and symbols are sensible signs that point to something beyond themselves that is both transcendent and incarnate: the incarnational oneness of the natural and supernatural, the human and divine (*Symbolic*). Indeed, Gioia has described his belief that "lyric poetry is both sacramental and metaphysical," that poets must hint at "what lies beyond the physical senses" (Snyder 127). As Felix Stefanile has put it, "In Cheever Country"—a "paean to our country's past and present business glories and defeats"—shows that "dream and transcend-ence can rise from such a cultural base" as corporate America (40).

The speaker in this poem spends his train ride watching from the "rattling / grime-streaked windows" the "landscape" none of the other commuters buried in books "takes too seriously." Unlike his fellow commuters, the speaker begins to see with vision and discloses the "poetry" in "the commonplace" (19), especially once "the sunset broadens" (20). This light, at once natural and sublime, invests the landscape and "passengers / standing on the platform" with a sense of the numinous. The ruined estates on the bluffs "glimmer in the river-brightened dusk." While sending warnings of human mutability, they still evoke "splendor," like the sun-suffused ruins in Turner's great romantic painting *Caernarvon Castle*. Gioia's speaker warms to the overlooked spirituality and imagines the "bright crowd" at the station of one town as living "an afterlife" (20). His imagination extends beyond the "gardens above the river" to "Somewhere up-state":

> huge factories melt ore,
> mills weave fabric on enormous looms,
> and sweeping combines glean the cash-green fields.
> Fortunes are made. Careers advance like armies.
> But here so little happens that is obvious. (21)

But he thinks also of balanced account books "and a hermit thrush" singing in an "unsold lot"; thus he realizes that though "here so little happens that is obvious," "in the odd light of a rainy afternoon" one can experience amid the ordinary what Wordsworth would call "the sense sublime." The images here recall Coleridge's "This Lime-Tree Bower My Prison." While watching the radiance of a sunset from his neighbor's tree-lined yard, the poet intuits that there is "No plot so narrow, be but Nature there." In the final stanza, then, Gioia's speaker similarly accepts his "ordinary town / where the lights on the hill" are "gleaming": it is a "modest" place and contains his life, but it's a place sanctified by love, home, and the light of imagination. This commuter appreciates his ecological niche.

Gioia studied Wordsworth with Herbert Lindenberger at Stanford, so it is no surprise that several poems show the poet's influence on his work. The form of "In Cheever Country" mutes the influence, for the poem is written in free verse with some iambic lines (as in stanza five), or in what Walzer calls "loose blank verse" (44), though many lines extend to fourteen syllables. The poem attempts a formal experiment—a free-verse poem that modulates into blank verse and then back again:

> The town names stenciled on the platform signs—
> Clear Haven, Bullet Park, and Shady Hill—
> show that developers at least believe in poetry
> if only as a talisman against the commonplace.
> There always seems so much to guard against. (19)

Here, only the first, second, and fifth lines scan as iambic pentameter. If Gioia had wanted to evoke *The Prelude* more obviously, he surely would have written in traditional blank verse, as Wordsworth does. Nevertheless, the romantic and sacramental sensibility of Wordsworth and Samuel Taylor Coleridge pervades the poem.

Two other poems present landscapes with sacramental potential. "California Hills in August" develops what April Lindner describes as Gioia's feeling of exile from his native state while living in the East, and indeed the poem turns on the opposite responses of easterners and natives to the late-summer terrain "already drained of green" where "the only other living thing / [is] a hawk, hungry for prey":

> An Easterner especially, who would scorn
> the meagerness of summer, the dry
> twisted shapes of black elm,
> scrub oak, and chaparral, a landscape
> August has already drained of green. (4)

But someone rooted to the place, "someone / raised in a landscape short of rain"—a California poet like Gioia—would view it as:

> the skyline of a hill broken by no more
> trees than one can count, the grass,
> the empty sky, the wish for water. (4).

The closing phrase turns what is "unbearable" into a hint of possible transcendence.

More explicit in its sacramental dimensions is "Song from a Courtyard Window." The dry Italian landscape depicted in this poem resembles the one in "California Hills," as Lindner astutely points out (29-30). Gioia describes in blank verse "a bitter landscape that two thousand years / of pastoral could not obscure or soften." Seated at a table in a crowded courtyard, "we" view:

> a wide dry field under the sun at noon
> where tall brown grass was bending in a wind
> filled with the sharp smell of a single weed
> that had marked this season here for centuries.
> The same wind drifting over the same land
> forever and forever. (60)

But this time what leads the speaker to intuit an under-presence in the landscape is not sight, but sound. Here the speaker and his companion listen to an "uncomprehending melody" sung by "a thirsty man" who is "somewhere out of sight." Simultaneously, "for a moment" they hear "nothing / but the rush of cool water underground / moving from the mountains to the hills / into these fountains splashing in the sun" (60). In the third verse-paragraph the speaker asks, "What did the vision mean?" He spends the rest of the poem contemplating how they were "woken up into the place from which / we've always woken out of," a "place" always "drifting / between the visible and invisible" (61). Though sure he experienced a vision—a sublime moment—he understands it was "A moment's pause, then nothing more," the same realization reached by the speaker in section V of "Daily Horoscope." Like so many Romantics, he is left with questions, not answers. "Only briefly," Gioia suggests, can we "see" into the life "of impenetrable things" (27).

THE GODS OF WINTER (1991)

Gioia's second collection, *The Gods of Winter*, followed closely on the heels of his translation of Eugenio Montale's *Mottetti: Poems of Love* (1990) and the brushfire he ignited in the *Atlantic Monthly*. Many critics found it superior to the first book. McPhillips calls the second book "no less diverse and satisfying" than *Daily Horoscope* and believes it secures Gioia's "permanent place in the canon" (Review 111, 114). Walzer agrees, stating that *The Gods of Winter* "moves beyond" the first collection and makes Gioia's cumulative "achievement" not only "substantial" but possibly enduring (46, 53). Nevertheless, coming in the wake of the controversial article, the new collection received scant attention in America compared to the widely noticed first book. *Daily Horoscope* drew more than two dozen reviews, most from prominent newspapers including the *New York Times* and major literary journals such as *Prairie Schooner, Poetry, Virginia Quarterly, New Criterion, Hudson Review, Sewanee Review,* and *Southern Humanities Review*. But *The Gods of Winter* managed just eighteen reviews in America, with only the last two publications listed above continuing to cover Gioia's work. In Britain, however, the book attained greater visibility; as the "Choice" of the Poetry Book Society—a distinction rarely awarded to Americans—*The Gods of Winter* received nearly as many reviews there, some in the most important sources, such as *TLS*. Though not all of the reviews were favorable—for instance, *TLS* critic Simon Carnell carped that the collection "is relatively long on rhetoric, short on telling detail" (9)—the reception to *The*

Gods proved on the whole strongly positive and lacked the hostility aimed at *Daily Horoscope*. For example, writing in *Poetry Wales*, Anne Stevenson praised *The Gods of Winter* as "important," fulfilling "the expectations raised by its form: a poetry of intuitive honesty that penetrates beyond appearances into possible aspects of the truth" (157-58). Affirming this positive reception was his winning, with Adrienne Rich, the 1992 Poets' Prize for best book of poetry.

The Gods of Winter encompasses elegies, dramatic monologues, topographical poems, and poems about poetry. It is a dark book, permeated by the death in December 1987 of the Gioias' first son, four-month-old Michael Jasper. The consequence of this trauma was a new vulnerability in Gioia's poetry. As he told Robert McPhillips, after the death, "I saw poetry differently. Writing took on a spiritual urgency I had never experienced before." He now wrote from "intuition and emotions," which means that he "wrote the poems that [his] life dictated" ("Dana" 26). His grief for the infant so transformed him that his suffering had made him "a different person," one newly "open to grace" (Koss 159). One result of this new emotional openness is several personal poems about death and grief. No doubt inspired by his mourning for his son, in "All Souls,'" Gioia imagines "that the dead can never leave the earth" since they are embedded in our environment, "silent as a rising mist" (4). Moreover, about the dead he says:

> They want their voices to become the wind—
> Intangible like them—to match its cry,
> Howling in treetops, covering the moon,
> Tumbling the storm clouds in a rain-swept sky. (4)

More directly personal are his elegies for his Uncle Theodore—who affected Gioia through the books he left behind—and for his son. Both poems center on the physical remains of the dead. In the opening stanza of "Night Watch," Gioia envisions his merchant-marine uncle on deck during his final voyage:

> I think of you standing on the sloping deck
> as the freighter pulls away from the coast of China,
> the last lights of Asia disappearing in the fog,
> and the engine's drone dissolving in the old
> monotony of waves slapping up against the hull. (5)

To end the poem, Gioia notes the irony that the sailor's "thin ashes have been buried" in the earth "and not scattered on the shifting gray Pacific" (6)—a line that clinches the free-verse poem with powerful restrained feeling.

The elegy to Michael, "Planting a Sequoia," is also in free verse, though this time the lines don't carry the ghost of pentameter, nor are they enjambed; instead, Gioia constructs a stanza of five end-stopped lines, longer than pentameter, with one line in the poem accommodating nineteen syllables. But the syllabic mass is well controlled, as each line encompasses a grammatical and syntactic whole, thus ensuring order and predictability. To illustrate, here is the first stanza where the speaker addresses the tree mentioned in the title:

> All afternoon my brothers and I have worked in the
> orchard,
> Digging this hole, laying you into it, carefully packing
> the soil.
> Rain blackened the horizon, but cold winds kept it over
> the Pacific,
> And the sky above us stayed the dull gray
> Of an old year coming to an end. (10)

It is expressive, too, that in each stanza the last line is considerably shorter. This diminishment reflects the infant boy's truncated life.

The poem also establishes a dignified order because the actions of the opening, we learn in the second stanza, represent an adaptation of Sicilian ritual. Just as fathers in the old country mark the birth of first sons by planting olive or fig trees, Gioia says he "would have done the same." But in the middle stanza the poem turns on the sad revelation that Gioia and his brothers are planting a sequoia—a tree native to the California soil of the family orchard—to commemorate not Michael's birth, but his death: "Defying the practical custom of our fathers," the brothers wrap "in [the tree's] roots a lock of hair, a piece of an infant's birth cord, / All that remains above earth of a first-born son" (10). The imagery of the poem entwines associations of beginnings and endings, referring to New Year's, "new fruit" in fall, and "a green sapling," as well as the "western light" of "the sunset." These implications beautifully prepare the reader for the graceful, moving conclusion, Gioia's hope for the tree's future:

> And when our family is no more, all of his unborn
>   brothers dead,
> Every niece and nephew scattered, the house torn down,
> His mother's beauty ashes in the air,
> I want you to stand among strangers, all young and
>   ephemeral to you,
> Silently keeping the secret of your birth. (10)

The poem is an apostrophe to the sequoia and illustrates Edward Hirsch's point that this direct address embraces "the archaic idea" of humanizing the nonhuman and appealing to it for help (36). Gioia, then, imagines that the tree, nourished by Michael's remains, will endure longer than the infant's generation, thereby symbolizing a form of immortality and remembrance, the long view of the Catholic perspective. As Janet McCann observes, "This poem illustrates the sacramental vision in and through the images of the family ritual and the broader implication that our acts have meaning, now and throughout time" (199). The poem, one of Gioia's best, "is one of the few entirely autobiographical poems" that he has "ever published" (Snyder 133). McPhillips contends that in Gioia's explicit, personal treatment of his son's death, the poem comes close to being "overtly confessional, albeit with supreme dignity" (New 50).

The blank-verse monologues concern death as well. "The Homecoming," which spans fourteen pages, adopts the blank verse of Frost, but as in Browning's dramatic monologues, it creates an arresting tension between judgment and sympathy. As in Browning's "My Last Duchess" and "Porphyria's Lover," in "Homecoming" the speaker is a murderer. He wins our sympathy and suspends our judgment, at least temporarily, even though in the twenty-fourth line he reveals to his silent listeners—the police and us—that he has committed mortal sin by killing his foster mother. The narrative develops depth of character through conversational speech and engaging details. The 408-line poem amounts to a confession that manifests the killer's "personal psychological profile," as Samuel Maio has observed; it "is a character study of someone who chooses evil" (71). The speaker tells the police—who have just arrived at his foster mother's home— that he was abandoned by both parents by age four. He grew up thinking his damnation was predestined:

> God didn't care. He saw where I belonged.
> [His foster mother] told me years ago how everyone
> would either go to Heaven or to Hell.
> God knew it all, and nothing you could do
> would make a difference. (41)

In the final lines, readers experience a *frisson* in moving from the mundane murder—"And I came up behind her all at once. / Then it was over"—to the killer's reaction, an epiphany of "happiness that went beyond my body" (51). In choosing evil, the speaker feels "free" (51). As Gioia explains, "The Homecoming" concerns "the choice of sin and the refusal of grace," "the nature of evil and free will" (Snyder 136). McPhillips suggests that "the most interesting moments of this poem involve the narrator's mystical rebirth into evil" (*New* 53). Maio rightfully calls this dramatic monologue Gioia's "consummate narrative" (72).

"Counting the Children" works as an interior monologue. The speaker, Mr. Choi, whose name echoes Gioia's, is an accountant called to take an inventory of a dead woman's estate and in the process discovers a room of dolls "salvaged from the trash" (14). He quotes the neighbor who leads him to them: " 'I want to show you hell' " (13). He then describes the dolls, using the tercet stanza of Dante's *Inferno*:

> Not a collection anyone would want—
> Just ordinary dolls salvaged from the trash
> With dozens of each kind all set together.
>
> Some battered, others missing arms and legs,
> Shelf after shelf of the same dusty stare
> As if despair could be assuaged by order. (14)

The internal rhyme of "stare" and "despair" subtly sets up the poem's psychological force. That night the speaker has a nightmare in which his daughter dies and he sees the dolls "screaming in the flames" (16).

We learn that when his daughter was young, Choi would check on her every night, "afraid of what" he "might discover" (16), fearing the crib death that took Dana and Mary Gioia's firstborn:

> And I remembered when she was a baby,
> How often I would get up in the night
> And creep into that room to watch her sleep.
>
> I never told my wife how many times
> I came to check each night—or that I was
> Always afraid of what I might discover.
>
> I felt so helpless standing by her crib,
> Watching the quiet motions of her breath
> In the half-darkness of the faint night-light. (16)

This fatherly protectiveness, and the universal fear of a parent's off-spring dying first, stems from Gioia's life as a new father; indeed, he had started the poem and was midway into section III when Michael died. About a year later, he resumed the poem and added section IV, which never would have been written if the infant had lived and which portrays Choi's vision of seeing "beyond my daughter to all children" (17), a vision like the one Gioia describes years later in "Special Treatments Ward." While "Counting the Children" embodies Gioia's grief, David Mason is right that only by adopting the mask of the monologue could Gioia write a poem of such potent, personal depth ("Other" 21).

The psychological representation of parental love is affecting, but Gioia's narrative also gives the accountant the kind of visionary moment normally noted only by poets. About "my vision," Choi states:

What I meant to ask is merely this:

What if completion comes only in beginnings?
The naked tree exploding into flower? (18)

He concludes that "We long for immortality, a soul / To rise up flaming from the body's dust" (18), the Catholic hope for redemption. Ultimately, while his vision seems to gesture to Plato and Wordsworth's "Ode: Intimations of Immortality," as Lindner intriguingly suggests (36), Choi believes that we gain immortality by unifying with our ancestors and with our children, "The ancient face returning in the child" (18). Thus he seems to invoke the Catholic belief in the communion of saints, the interconnection of the living and the dead. As in Dante, Gioia has said that in "Counting the Children" Choi journeys to hell but at the end has "a glimpse into paradise" (Snyder 134). Nevertheless, the monologue ends hauntingly, with Choi confused and disturbed that his daughter has lined up her own dolls on a shelf. This ending represents the best unspoken subtext in Gioia's repertoire.

The narratives occupy parts II and IV; parts III and V contain works on landscape, both rural and urban, and on poetry itself. In part III, "Rough Country" resembles "California Hills in August" from *Daily Horoscope*, with the speaker preferring "a landscape made of obstacles," "a spot so hard to reach that no one comes" (23)—perhaps especially easterners. "Becoming a Redwood" in part V similarly betrays Gioia's attachment to his native ground and exhibits what Jonathan Bate would call "ecopoesis," the poetry that sings the song of the earth and creates a path to "the place of dwelling" (75-76). Both these poems exemplify Gioia's roots as a California poet. Conversely, the final poem in the book concerns an urban landscape and is as fine a lyric as Gioia has written. Unlike "Becoming a Redwood," "Equations of the Light" evokes in blank verse a "discovered" place whose atmosphere supplies a spot of time:

> The streetlamps splashed the shadows of the leaves
> across the whitewashed brick, and each tall window
> glowing through the ivy-decked facade
> promised lives as perfect as the light. (61)

But as in the poems about heightened "moments" in *Daily Horoscope*, this moment too ends:

> Traffic bellowed from the avenue.
> Our shadows moved across the street's long wall,
> and at the end what else could I have done
> but turn the corner back into my life? (62)

It is as if Gioia is suggesting that moments of spiritual awareness gain their meaning through our human limitations. As he says in "The Burning Ladder," the initial poem in *Daily Horoscope*, "Gravity / always greater than desire" (3).

Finally, three poems about poetry provide the volume with some relief. "The Silence of the Poets" sarcastically presents a time when poets have "stopped writing," freeing "busy people" to enjoy the distractions of "progress" (30). The underlying connections to *Can Poetry Matter?* are clear as the poem depicts the cultural problem this collection of essays tries to address: "the decline of poetry's cultural importance" and "the divorce of poetry from the educated reader" ("Can" 3, 9). "My Confessional Sestina" skewers another bête noir of Gioia's, university creative writing programs. The poem satirizes workshops populated by students "who care less about being poets than contributors" (31) and are likely to become contributors who do not read the "small magazines" that publish them ("Can" 6). "The Next Poem," the best of the trio, is an *ars poetica*. It lays out what Gioia the poet rejects:

> No jumble box of imagery
> dumped glumly in the reader's lap
> or elegantly packaged junk
> the unsuspecting must unwrap.

And what he aspires to:

> words that could direct a friend
> precisely to an unknown place,
> those few unshakeable details
> that no confusion can erase.

> And the real subject left unspoken
> but unmistakable to those
> who don't expect a jungle parrot
> in the black and white of prose. (34-35)

"The Next Poem" is one of five in *The Gods of Winter* written in rhymed quatrains. The book is Gioia's most spare, but every poem, formal or free, is honed and telling.

INTERROGATIONS AT NOON (2001)

Gioia's third book of poems, *Interrogations at Noon*, vividly reconfirms the poet's range of styles and subjects and supports his general aim to be "a poet who tries to do a good job" by exploring "the full resources" of "the English language." It deservedly won the 2002 American Book Award for Poetry. Some critics, however, delivered mixed judgments. The reviewer for *Publishers Weekly* lauded the songs from *Nosferatu* "for their verve" and underscored that Gioia's "real gift" lies in "light verse"; nevertheless, Gioia gets blamed for predictability and for failing "to make" his poems about ordinary life "linguistically or emotionally compelling in any way" (Review of *Interrogations*). Without fully understanding Gioia's metrical intentions, Arthur Mortensen alternated praise for Gioia's "well-wrought" verse with some nitpicking about lines that have "an odd feel" and "slippery prosody," but the critic finally recommends the "not always satisfying collection" because "it has some solid, well-written poems" ("Brief Look"). In contrast, Leslie Monsour considered Gioia's poems about loss to be successful "because the poems are genuine" and infused "with a style and beauty that is much too rare" ("O Dark"). And in my own review in *American Book Review*, I concluded that *Interrogations* is "a strong and varied collection," both "well-crafted and often moving" ("Midlife" 17).

Gioia's stylistic range perhaps shows strongest in the free-verse poems. Of the seven poems in the first part, two are in free verse and a third, "The Litany," modulates in and out of blank verse. "Elegy with Surrealist Proverbs as Refrain"—the least characteristic poem in the collection but typical of Gioia's modernist vein—fittingly follows no set metrical pattern, which is why Mortensen laments the "absence" in the poem of "a strong meter" ("Brief Look"). But it is typical of Gioia's free verse in its discipline; Gioia shapes the poem into four eight-line stanzas. Moreover, as in Gioia's other forays into free verse, in "Elegy" the rhythms are only relatively loose, for many of its lines scan as perfect iambs, despite its irrational juxtapositions of ideas and images; in fact, some lines fittingly echo the twelve-syllable alexandrine of French verse:

> Bre*ton* / con*sid* /ered *su* /*icide* / the *tru* /est *art*,
> though *life* / seemed *hard* /ly *worth* / the *troub* /le *to* / dis*card*. (8)

Or, frequently, as in "Time Travel," a line will meet Frost's criterion of loose iambic pentameter. Coming after a line we can scan as iambic tetrameter and another as iambic pentameter with a medial pyrrhic, the third line below scans as a headless hexameter, a headless foot and then five iambs:

> How *long* it *took* to *recognize*
> The *shameless modesty* of *our* de*sire*—
> *Only to* pos*sess* what *we* al*ready* had. (65)

Gioia's nuanced attention to rhythm here reflects his goal to make the new collection "musical" (Baer 42), and by providing stylistic variety, it helps the book appeal to a range of readers.

The poem that opens the book, "Words," may read like free verse, but it actually conforms to a five-stress line. Written in lines as long as fifteen syllables, it exemplifies Gioia's experiments with meter. He begins:

> The world does not need words. It articulates itself
> in sunlight, leaves, and shadows. The stones on the path
> are no less real for lying uncatalogued and uncounted.
> The fluent leaves speak only the dialect of pure being.
> The kiss is still fully itself though no words were spoken. (3)

Then the poem unveils the essential need of humans for poetic utterance: "To name is to know and remember" (3). Language thus affirms the organic world even though it is ultimately unpossessable, its beauty indifferent, "greater than ourselves and all the airy words we summon" (3). The well-wrought stanzas manifest the suggestion that our redemption lies in our representations and memory of this greater world, which help connect us to it, however tenuously. In "Words," Gioia deliberately counters the postmodern mistrust of language as having "no exact relationship with reality" by creating a poem about the "Catholic sense of the relationship between language and the world" (Koss 160), which for a Christian boils down to "the relation between the visible and the invisible" (Snyder 127).

Even when Gioia resorts to traditional forms, he exercises great flexibility. Thirteen poems incorporate blank verse, including the translations of Seneca, "Descent to the Underworld" and "Juno Plots Her Revenge." "Juno" supplies this volume's middle-length narrative. Gioia's meter helps bring the Roman playwright Seneca to life, rendering Juno's shamed and angry monologue with dramatic intensity and vivid colloquiality. Addressing the Furies, Juno implores:

> Come to me, sisters, with your hair aflame,
> With savage claws. Inflict your punishments.
> Revenge the desecration of the Styx.
> Shatter his sanity. Make his *soul burn*
> And make me mad as well, *blind*ed by hate,
> Senseless with anger, famished for his blood. (47; my emphasis)

Well-placed metrical substitutions, such as the spondee "soul burn" and the trochaic reversal of rhythm in "blinded," seamlessly reinforce Juno's shifting, barely controlled feelings. And though modulated to accommodate Juno's conversational voice, the blank verse here at times rings with sonic effects. Two examples are the long *o*'s and *r*'s in "But the gross trophy of Europa's rape!"—and the *w*'s, *m*'s, and long *o*'s in "those nymphs / Who terrorize the waves, once warmed Jove's bed" (43).

Gioia handles blank verse with equal finesse in "The Voyeur." This poem introduces the theme repeated later in the book in "Entrance"—that the way forward from an irretrievable past and a deadened present is to recognize that our "eyes . . . have forgotten how to see / from viewing things already too well-known" (15). In "The Voyeur," Gioia presents a husband imagining himself "suspended in the branches by the window, / entering this strange bedroom with his eyes" and "watching" his wife "undress." Later, the husband "hears a woman singing in the shower," and "The branches shake their dry leaves like alarms." This pentameter line ends the wry poem perfectly, both through the humorous yet resonant simile and through the rhythmic intensity of its clustered stresses (in "their *dry / leaves like / alarms*") (4). Like Seamus Heaney's "The Skunk," Gioia's "The Voyeur" is a memorable marriage poem about taking things for granted and needing to wipe the film of familiarity from our eyes.

Despite the musical effectiveness in blank verse, in *Interrogations*, Gioia increases his reliance on both rhymed stanzas and non-iambic meters. As he told William Baer in an interview for the *Formalist*, he welcomes "metrical diversity." "I've often felt," Gioia said, "that the New Formalism could have been called the 'New Iambicism'" (42). A third of the new poems rhyme, and these works exploit couplets and the ballad rhyme scheme (*abcb*) in a variety of meters. "At the Waterfront Café," for instance, uses both forms, alternating quatrains of couplets (four stresses per half line) with ballad stanzas in long meter (four stresses per line). Through this form suitable to light verse, Gioia entertainingly pokes gentle fun at the rich and trendy:

> Docked beside the quiet river, yachts are rocking in the
>   sun
> While their skippers stop for cocktails to replay the
>   race they've run.
> Military in their khakis, they invade the chic café.
> Smirnoff tinkles in their tumblers. No one's drinking
>   Perrier.
>
> In the parking lot a valet
> Sunbathes by a sleek Mercedes

Till he's prodded by a matron
For directions to the Ladies'. (37)

More biting in its satire is "The Archbishop," written "for a famous
critic." In quatrains containing three-beat lines, it exposes the pomp-
ous hypocrisy of a prelate, an implied metaphor for a critic:

The Archbishop declines to wear glasses,
So his sense of the world grows dim.
He thinks that the crowds at Masses
Have gathered in honor of him. (30)

The sixth quatrain underlines the Archbishop's vanity:

While high in the chancery office
His Reverence studies the glass,
Wondering which of his vestments
Would look best at Palm Sunday Mass. (30)

Some critics have translated the archbishop as Harold Bloom, but
Helen Vendler is perhaps the more likely target. Or, given that
Marjorie Perloff has multiple times singled out Gioia for attacks,
even calling him "untalented," she could be the bull's-eye as well.

Among other accessible rhyming lyrics are three songs from
Gioia's libretto *Nosferatu* and "Summer Storm." For instance,
"Nosferatu's Serenade" ("Aria: Nosferatu's Nocturne" in the libretto)
communicates a *frisson* in quatrains composed of two rhyming
couplets in lines of four accented syllables. Gioia opens the poem
with this quatrain:

I am the image that darkens your glass,
The shadow that falls wherever you pass.
I am the dream you cannot forget,
The face you remember without having met.

45

And here is how he ends the poem:

> You've heard me inside you speak in your dreams,
> Sigh in the ocean, whisper in streams.
> I am the future you crave and you fear.
> You know what I bring. Now I am here. (33)

These eight lines provide telling words for the unspoken but vivid images of Murnau's silent film.

For "Summer Storm," Gioia constructs a quatrain in ballad meter that rhymes the second and fourth lines. The love lost and regretted in "Summer Storm" is less substantial than in "My Dead Lover," never having really lived at all, except in the speaker's mind. But twenty years after a chance and brief meeting at a wedding reception, he wonders about "that evening's memory / Return[ing] with this night's storm" (66), and he finally confronts the seeming arbitrariness of any life's plot:

> There are so many *might-have-beens*,
> *What-ifs* that won't stay buried,
> Other cities, other jobs,
> Strangers we might have married. (67)

Then, Gioia closes the poem with an adroit offbeat rhyme that undercuts the senseless but unavoidable pining of memory:

> And memory insists on pining
> For places it never went,
> As if life would be happier
> Just by being different. (67)

The concluding rhyme of "went" and "different" can be read two ways. While most readers would recite the final syllable of "different" as a promoted stress (*diff*-er-*ent*), thus achieving a true rhyme, pronouncing the word as one might in speech—with the last syllable unstressed (*diff*-rent)—captures the speaker's sense of a missed connection.

In addition to versatility of style, *Interrogations* comprises a range of subjects. "Words for Music" includes enjoyable light verse, and the two narratives adapted from Seneca tell animated stories from classical mythology. A frequent topic here is love, written about with the subjectivity of autobiography, even if the results are fictional. In "Notes on the New Formalism," Gioia identifies "the bankruptcy of the confessional mode" as one source of contemporary poetry's troubles (41). More recently, he describes short autobiographical poems as "*exactly* the kinds of poems" he avoided as models when he began to write seriously. Prizing "critical distance and objectivity," he still claims to "have written almost no directly autobiographical poems" (Baer 29-30). And yet a large number of the lyrics in *Interrogations* treat personal if not directly confessional or autobiographical subjects, and these poems, significantly, represent the book's greatest strength.

The lyrics of midlife regret encompass marriage, love, and once more the death of Gioia's firstborn son. "Spider in the Corner" employs a first-person plural point of view; its domestic details reverberate with the authenticity of personal experience or observation:

> Another day of books and spoiled plans,
> of cigarettes and sitting still
> in rooms too small for us. How little there
>
> is left to talk about except the weather.
> And so we tolerate the silence
> like the spider in the corner neither one
>
> of us will kill. Yes, the doorway whispers.
> But we will stay—until the weather clears,
> the endless rain that keeps us here together. (63)

More direct are the first-person poems in which the persona speaks about old lovers: "Summer Storm," "Corner Table," and "My Dead Lover," whose blank-verse quatrains mourn a woman whose "body was the first I ever knew / Better than my own" but who now is "nothing, / Not even ashes" (53). Unquestionably autobiographical—and emotionally powerful—are the other lyrics of grief. Like "Planting a Sequoia" and "All Souls' " in *The Gods of Winter*, "Pentecost," "Metamorphosis," and "The Litany" address Dana and Mary Gioia's ongoing love and loss of what he calls "my lesion" (11), their son Michael Jasper. A believer in the communion of saints, Gioia has said his "deepest relationships are mostly with the dead" (Koss 171). "The Lost Garden" also elegiacally addresses the past but finds redemption in memory: "The trick," Gioia discovers, "is making memory a blessing." This trick means, he writes in beautifully rendered blank verse, "wanting nothing more than what has been" and simultaneously—despite knowing "the past" is "forever lost"—"seeing / Behind the wall a garden still in blossom" (68). In our fallen world, memory can be a blessing because it "and imagination," Gioia maintains, "constitute our human means of conquering time and mortality" (Snyder 149).

In lyric after lyric, then, Gioia writes with open emotion controlled in well-crafted lines and stanzas that carefully balance feeling and form. James Merrill once remarked that preserving "the lyric impulse during the middle years is no easy matter" (qtd. in Vendler 101). In *Interrogations* the then-fifty-year-old poet maintained and strengthened his lyricism. The result is a moving, engaging volume whose core is lyrical and personal, but whose compass includes various forms, subjects, and tones.

PITY THE BEAUTIFUL (2012)

In the wake of publishing *Interrogations at Noon*, Gioia's poetic output slowed. Nevertheless, he published more critical essays and another opera libretto. He brought out two new collections of criticism, *Barrier of a Common Language* and *Disappearing Ink*, and he contributed the libretto to *Tony Caruso's Final Broadcast*. He also, of course, devoted his time to leading the National Endowment for the Arts. This service cost him seven years as a poet, and he feared he might never publish another book of poems (Johnson 35). Finally, after an eleven-year gap, Graywolf Press released Gioia's fourth collection of poems, *Pity the Beautiful*. It is a work mostly of continuities with his earlier poetry and forms a worthy addition to his canon. All of Gioia's first four books divide into five parts containing poems in free verse and in meter and sometimes rhyme. Like *Interrogations at Noon*, *Pity* commits one part to "Words for Music," including four songs from *Tony Caruso's Final Broadcast*, and as in both *Interrogations* and *The Gods of Winter*, the new book features a long narrative, "Haunted," that fills an entire section. Other carryovers include poems evoking Gioia's dead son, translations (this time of Mario Luzi and Bartolo Cattafi), and love poems.

Though a decade separates *Pity the Beautiful* from *Interrogations at Noon*, Gioia opens the new volume seamlessly as "The Present" echoes and develops the theme of the poem that closes *Interrogations*, "Unsaid." "Unsaid" juxtaposes what we confide to what we conceal:

> So much of what we live goes on inside—
> The diaries of grief, the tongue-tied aches
> Of unacknowledged love are no less real
> For having passed unsaid. What we conceal
> Is always more than what we dare confide.
> Think of the letters that we write our dead. (69)

"The Present" revives the subject of concealed feelings but goes beyond merely describing this emotional reality and promotes the virtue of keeping things "inside":

> The present that you gave me months ago
> is still unopened by our bed,
> sealed in its rich blue paper and bright bow.
> I've even left the card unread
> and kept the ribbon knotted tight.
> Why needlessly unfold and bring to light
> the elegant contrivances that hide
> the costly secret waiting still inside? (3)

"The Present," then, repeats the subject of "Unsaid" that our inner lives are real even if unrevealed. Gioia suggests the same thing in "Lonely Impulse of Delight," his autobiographical essay. Here he observes, "our inner lives are as rich and real as our outer lives, even if they remain mostly unknowable to others" (1). But "The Present" argues that it is best to leave "the card unread" and the gift "sealed" in its "elegant contrivances" since what's "inside" is "the costly secret." It's better, the poem tells us, to keep "the ribbon knotted tight," to keep "the diaries of grief" and regret "unsaid." Whereas "Unsaid" unfolds in conversational blank verse, Gioia aptly contrives a more elegant, formal pattern for "The Present," combining tetrameter and pentameter lines woven in a scheme that rhymes *ababccdd*. In fact, in its form and its approach to its topic, the non-confessional "Present" embodies Gioia's desire to "cut out a great deal of what I once would have left in a poem" (Johnson 28). It also invites us to read into it Gioia's poetic aim to avoid the confessional.

Other poems confront this theme of the cost of hiding, or revealing, what goes on inside. "The Argument" begins with "you" putting "the phone down," leaving your rebuttal left unsaid as "the words" on the other end "don't vanish all at once." The poem builds on this synecdoche of the caller's words representing him or her and dramatizes the effect on the "you" of what the caller should have kept "inside" and "unsaid." Even the next day, the poem concludes about words, you can:

> Listen to them rage above the quiet road,
> Screeching out their righteousness
> A*long* the *miles* of *tight-strung wire*. (61; my emphasis)

This free-verse lyric centered on an extended metaphor ends with a tense resonance and an expressive string of accented words, three of them repeating the long *i* sound.

"The Apple Orchard," in blank-verse tercets, supplies still another view on holding in our feelings. It narrates a time the first-person speaker and the woman he addresses walked beneath the arching branches of apple trees that formed "spring's ephemeral cathedral." They were "in love but never lovers," so the speaker assumes the woman "won't remember" this "April afternoon." For him, however, it's a spot of time, a moment when he felt "The *bright flame burn*ing," a phrase charged with stressed syllables (my emphasis). Yet most memorable to the speaker is the cost he has paid ever since by concealing his secret, what in "Unsaid" he calls "the tongue-tied aches / Of unacknowledged love":

> Nothing consumed, such secrets brought to light!
> There was a moment when I stood behind you,
> Reached out to spin you toward me . . . but I stopped.
>
> What more could I have wanted from that day?
> Everything, of course. (57)

The poem ends with a didactic lesson: "the point," Gioia asserts, is "To learn that what we will not grasp is lost" (57). So, "The Apple Orchard" supplies a case when the bow should have been untied and the hidden feelings exposed.

If *Pity the Beautiful* opens with a warning about revealing what we hide inside, Gioia nevertheless writes about his family in three of the book's better poems, all autobiographical. In "Unsaid" he suggests we mentally write letters to "our dead"; "Finding a Box of Family Letters" is about Gioia wanting "to send a postcard / to the underworld" (18). It is a letter to the dead that does get said. The tone stays light, implying an acceptance that his father is gone, while still expressing the son's abiding love. "My father breaks my heart," Gioia writes, "simply by being so young and handsome." In letters written during the war, "He says he misses all of us / (though I haven't yet been born)." Gioia admits, "It's silly to get sentimental," but in perusing a photo from "a banquet sixty years ago," he considers what the band was playing and implores his parents, "*Get out there on the floor and dance! / You don't have forever.*" The poem is written in free verse, which makes it seem spontaneous and tender. The ending is lighthearted, touching, and clever, but also serious in pushing the theme of *carpe diem* (as does "The Apple Orchard") and our need to realize that our lives are temporary:

> It's silly to get sentimental.
> The dead have moved on. So should we.
> But isn't it equally simpleminded to miss
> the special expertise of the departed
> in clarifying our long-term plans?
>
> They never let us forget that the line
> between them and us is only temporary.
> *Get out there and dance!* the letters shout
> adding, *Love always. Can't wait to get home!*
> And soon we will be. *See you there.* (19)

These pious feelings—the product of grief—no doubt needed time before they could be "said"; indeed, the poem affirms that "The dead have moved on. So should we" (19). Still, the poem reminds us that Gioia's "deepest relationships are mostly with the dead" (Koss 171). Gioia recasts this theme in the book's last poem, "Majority," where he discovers "it makes sense" at last that his son, who now would be twenty-one, has "moved away / into [his] own afterlife" (68). In sparse quatrains, Gioia relates what has been unsaid until the poem's unfolding. Its restraint—and recognition of the truth—is moving.

The other poem about Gioia as a father, and the subject of expressing deep feelings in words, is "Special Treatments Ward," one of his most powerful poems. David Mason calls it "masterly" and "one of the best things he has written in years" ("Inner" 146). This poem manifests "tongue-tied" "diaries of grief," the struggle to forget them, and the ultimate pressure to say what needs saying in a poem the poet does not choose to write but must. Gioia structures the poem in three sections, each in iambic pentameter, but each section consists of diminishing length and stanza size. In section I, in three seven-line stanzas with occasional rhyme, Gioia charts a narrative from more than a decade before about a surviving son's stay in a "hospital's highest floor," "where the children come to die":

> They wear their bandages like uniforms
> and pull their IV rigs along the hall
> with slow and careful steps. Or bald and pale,
> they lie in bright pajamas on their beds,
> watching another world on a screen. (29)

At night "the mothers" at last "slip / beside their children, as if they might mesh / those small bruised bodies back into their flesh." The second stanza ends with the heartbreaking truth that despite "love so strong," "Each morning proves [the mothers] wrong." These stanzas define the parents' anguish: "We need to talk," Gioia admits, but "There is a word that no one ever speaks" (29). As Gioia writes in "Unsaid," the closing poem in *Interrogations at Noon*, "What we conceal / Is always more than what we dare confide"; and what we conceal, the poem suggests, are "diaries of grief," "letters that we write our dead," or soon-to-be dead.

Though the first section might function as a complete poem on its own, the other two sections deepen it in striking ways. Section II, a set of four quatrains, opens with the most personal statement in Gioia's entire body of work. He says,

> I put this poem aside twelve years ago
> because I could not bear remembering
> the faces it evoked. (30)

He next admits more intimate motives:

> What right had I whose son had walked away
> to speak for those who died? And I'll admit
> I wanted to forget. I'd lost one child
> and couldn't bear to watch another die. (30)

He couldn't find words to stitch "shut these wounds" and thus abandoned the poem, but he realized that "there are poems we do not choose to write."

And because poets must write these poems, years later he resumed writing his autobiographical poem, creating section III. Here he crafts four tercets and a solitary final line that vividly present what he can't forget, "The children" who "visit" him, "not just in dream." These lines remind us of Mr. Choi in "Counting the Children" and borrow its form; only here, in "Special Treatments Ward," Gioia takes off the mask of the monologue and speaks directly from the heart:

> A few I recognize, untouched by years.
> I cannot name them—their faces pale and gray
> like ashes fallen from a distant fire.

> What use am I to them, almost a stranger?
> I cannot wake them from their satin beds. (31)

He "cannot name them," the poet's archetypal job, and "cannot wake them from their satin beds." And while he finally has untied his tongue to write this "diary of grief," the children "never speak," like the nightmarish dolls in "Counting" (31). "Special Treatments Ward" is unquestionably one of Gioia's best poems and his most confessional. He finds a way here to redeem what he once called "the bankruptcy of the confessional mode" ("Notes" 41).

If some poems revolve around what to conceal and what to reveal, others search for declarative resolutions, as in "The Apple Orchard," but end with questions (as does "Special Treatments Ward": "Why do they seek me?"). In "The Coat" the speaker thinks he sees a woman he knows because she is "wearing your coat." After following her to the subway where she disappears like Persephone, the speaker asks a series of questions about this ghost and her warning, wondering if "the coat itself" had "come simply to taunt me / With the fragrance of spring on a cold, dead morning?" (60). This poem ends suggestively by balancing the elusive "fragrance" of hope (or the missed vitality of the past) and the weather of winter. "The Road" and "Cold San Francisco"—Gioia's two sonnets (his first that rhyme)—both end with questions. The latter sonnet from "The Words for Music" part is effective. It inventively employs a four-beat line with an anapestic lilt, as well as slant rhymes that reinforce a lack of connection: "We shall go to the house where we buried the years, / Where the door is locked, and we haven't a key" (47). Similarly, "Reunion" uses rhymed quatrains to dramatize the disorientation of reentering one's past but being unable to name one's friends, leading the speaker to ask, "Or is confusion all I can feel?" (8). So, if some of Gioia's poems include declarative statements, many others conclude with unanswered questions.

What's new in *Pity* are poems showing Gioia's widening interest in religion and in particular Catholicism as an overt poetic subject.

Like earlier titles—"Prayer" and "Pentecost," for instance—some poems are serious, such as the dramatic monologue "The Angel with the Broken Wing" and "Prayer at Winter Solstice," which in end-stopped, free-verse couplets presents a series of beatitudes:

> Blessed are the saint and the sinner who redeem each other.
> Blessed are the dead, calm in their perfection.
>
> Blessed is the pain that humbles us.
> Blessed is the distance that bars our joy.
>
> Blessed is this shortest day that makes us long for light.
> Blessed is the love that in losing we discover. (17)

But others are comic or satirical. "The Seven Deadly Sins" adopts the voice of Pride, who sneers at his six companions:

> Hell, we're not even done, and Anger
> is already arguing about the bill.
> I'm the only one who
> ever leaves a decent tip.
>
> Let them all go, the losers!
> It's a relief to see Sloth's
> fat ass go out the door. (26)

Though humorous, the poem yet expresses Gioia's Catholic world-view of humankind's fallen state, which includes evil and sin as well as the need for redemption. "Shopping" and "The Freeways Considered as Earth Gods" adroitly sling their mock-heroic stanzas in long end-stopped lines. "Shopping" elevates the mall to temple, and the speaker implores its gods—including "Mercury, protector of cell phones and fax machines" (10)—to "Sing" him "the hymns of no cash down and the installment plan." Yet, at the end, the speaker cannot find his "errant soul" in the fallen world of consumerism. In the closing lines he thinks he glimpses her "behind the greasy window of the bus" vanishing in rush-hour traffic (11-12).

These clever, satiric poems about the gods bring a new diction to Gioia's poems, but new too is the narrative that comprises the middle part of *Pity*. "Haunted" is a ghost story entwined with a love story, organized in short blank-verse paragraphs. It adopts many Gothic conventions and influences, such as the narrative frame that readers don't fully figure out until the end of the poem, where we learn that the speaker is a monk delivering to a bar bottles of brandy he's vinted and distilled himself; a bartender acts as the monologue's silent listener, or perhaps a confessor of sorts. The poem also invokes Lovecraft, a writer from Gioia's boyhood, but further reminds one of Poe's "Ligeia"—in its mixture of horror and macabre eroticism—and perhaps of Madeline from "The Fall of the House of Usher." In a distant wing of a vacated mansion, the speaker encounters what at first he takes as "a handsome woman in her early forties." It's funny that he "didn't want to scare her" (39), but soon he admits to himself that she seems like a ghost:

> So how did I address this revenant,
> this traveler from the undiscovered country,
> who stared at me with dark, unblinking eyes?
> I caught my breath, got on my feet, and said—
> nothing at all. The words stuck in my throat.
>
> We stood there face to face, inches apart.
> Her pale skin shined like a window catching sunlight,
> both bright and clear, but chilling to the touch.
> She stared at me with undisguised contempt,
> and then she whispered, almost in a hiss,
> "You don't belong here. No, you don't belong here." (40-41)

The monk-to-be (who ironically recalls Matthew Lewis's protagonist-priest in the Gothic potboiler *The Monk*) has been spending the weekend in this country manor with Mara, a beauty "slightly evil" to fall in love with. At first he chooses to be her "accomplice" rather than her "victim," but he ends up neither (35). When he flees the ghost to return to Mara's side, he notices their hearts beating out of sync, so he realizes that what the ghost has told him rings with truth, "*I don't belong here*" (41); consequently, he flees the house, like the narrator at the end of "The Fall of the House of Usher."

The intricately layered story can be enjoyed on just its literal level, but as with any good work of Gothic literature, the psychological underpinnings invite interpretation. For one thing, the monk's new religious life—embracing "Poverty, Chastity, and Growing Grapes" (42)—compensates for what Mara represents and what she wants to seduce the narrator into accepting: a world of luxury, sex, and the constant pursuit of "peak moments" (35). The critique of hedonism and excess ends lightly, though, for the monk tells the barkeep it's the life here, not the afterlife, that he doesn't "want to waste": he is known for his miraculous port (42). Earlier he marveled at Mara's uncle's collection of "legendary" labels—so "prodigal" and vast the uncle "could have entertained / Napoleon and half his *Grande Armée*" (37). "Haunted" is well paced, with vivid descriptions, and the narrator's voice, conversational like a seasoned storyteller's, is well fitted to blank verse.

Pity the Beautiful includes other fine poems, in particular the love poem "After a Line of Neruda" and the lyrics to "Marketing Department Trio," the first song from *Tony Caruso's Final Broadcast*. Altogether the book confirms Gioia's hallmark diversity of subjects and styles and develops his identity as a Catholic poet. Thus it forms a sturdy addition to his poetic edifice. Kevin T. O'Connor finds in *Pity* Gioia's recurring "virtues" of "subtle music and insight" (Review), and Bruce Bawer describes Gioia as "an authentic virtuoso" for exercising "perfect control over" the "emotional depths" his poems embody. Bawer even goes so far as to second the lofty judgment on the back cover that Gioia has become "a classic poet" (336).

99 POEMS: NEW & SELECTED (2016)

In 2016, Graywolf Press brought out *99 Poems: New & Selected*. It represents the culmination of Gioia's poetic career. With the poetry wars long dead, critics responded uniformly with high praise. *Publishers Weekly*, which fifteen years earlier had received *Interrogations at Noon* poorly, now raved about Gioia's "immense talents," his "careful diction and dedication to the line." In summation, the anonymous critic refers to Gioia as a "master poet" (Review). In a review full of insights into Gioia's poetry, James Matthew Wilson goes even further, hailing Gioia "as one of the great Catholic poets of the last century" ("In Christ-Haunted"). In yet another favorable assessment, Stephen Massamilla praises Gioia's "mastery of many genres and forms" but especially admires his narratives in which Gioia unspools "his lines with Audenesque clarity and wit" ("Achievement"). In a review in *Able Muse*, Brooke Clark similarly holds Gioia's handling of blank-verse narrative in high regard, singling out the new narrative "Style" for its sharp storytelling and nimble iambic pentameter (97). Overall, despite her "quibble" with the New Formalism, Clark argues that *99 Poems* places Gioia among "the finest poets of his era" (97). A. M. Juster concurs, regarding the book "an important collection by an important poet" ("Case").

To compile his selected poems, Gioia employed a novel scheme. Poets almost always organize such collections chronologically. Ted Kooser's *Sure Signs* (1980) is a notable exception, its poems forming an unbroken sequence without sections nor any indications where individual poems originated. In *99 Poems*, Gioia similarly foregoes chronology; however, unlike Kooser, Gioia arranges his poems by subject, slotting them into seven categories: Mystery, Place, Remembrance, Imagination, Stories, Songs, and Love. This approach makes the volume less like a retrospective than a new book with an order that creates fresh interconnections between the poems. Readers eager to trace Gioia's development book to book still can do so by checking the index that identifies the textual origin of each poem. One advantage of the thematic emphasis is that it gives a stronger sense of the unity and cohesion of Gioia's canon, and it also serves better as an introduction to new audiences. As in any selected volume, Gioia has culled his four collections to preserve his best work. Whereas he weeded out nearly half of the poems in his first book, *Daily Horoscope*, he omitted just five from his second, *The Gods of Winter*, the volume for which he shared the Poets' Prize with Adrienne Rich. Many of the poems he cut from the next two books are translations, versions, or songs from libretti. All these deletions help the strongest, most original poems stand out. Altogether the arrangement underscores the consistency in quality and in theme throughout Gioia's canon.

The fifteen new poems reinforce the diversity of subject and style in Gioia's work and include some of his better poems. Formally, one-third employ stanzaic free verse, a fraction consistent throughout his thirty years of published collections; one-fifth rhyme; and while four poems embody accentual meters, both rhymed as in "Film Noir" and "Household Gods" and unrhymed as in "Monster," another quartet unfold in blank verse. The new poems vary in type, too. "Style" is a long narrative in the mold of his dramatic monologues such as "Haunted," "Sea Pebbles" is an elegy, "Household Gods" amusing light verse comparable to "Pity the Beautiful," and "Homage to Soren Kierkegaard" a blank-verse character sketch akin to "Elegy for Vladimir de Pachmann." This variety in manner parallels the range in subject matter. Gioia adds between one and three poems to each of his seven thematic sections, including three each on Place, Imagination, and Love. These new works, then, fit seamlessly into the selected poems reprinted in *99 Poems*.

A few new poems stand out as equal to his previous best. "Marriage of Many Years," which concludes the volume, is the poem Gioia points to as best summing up his values. "It's a love poem to my wife," he notes, "but it is also about language, imagination and mortality" (qtd. in Salai). Unlike "The Voyeur," another poem about marriage but one that adopts a humorous and almost creepy point of view to make a serious point, "Marriage of Many Years" maintains a serious tone, even if it too evokes the sensuality of conjugal love. Its two eight-line stanzas in blank verse convey heft, even while the lines flow like part of a tender conversation. It celebrates the long view, the intimacy of marriage and its uniqueness to a couple bonded until death:

> Most of what happens happens beyond words.
> The lexicon of lip and fingertip
> defies translation into common speech.
> I recognize the musk of your dark hair.
> It always thrills me, though I can't describe it.
> My finger on your thigh does not touch skin—
> it touches your skin warming to my touch.
> You are a language I have learned by heart. (188)

Ultimately, it is about the commitment that lasts until they face "what must be lost" (188), till death does them part. What must be lost is not just their "lexicon of lip and fingertip," the "patois" spoken by them alone, but also their "sovereign secrecy" that makes them like a "tribe of two" whose language of the heart faces extinction (188). The poem revives Gioia's theme of language beyond words, of meaning inhering as much in what's unsaid as in the words we use to name the world. His feelings for his wife defy "translation" and description. Moreover, this extended metaphor of the couple as a tribe whose native tongue will die with them enacts Gioia's poetics of imagination, his belief in the incarnational beauty of language.

"Sea Pebbles: An Elegy" and "Vultures Mating" excel as poems of place. The elegy opens by addressing an unidentified but still mourned "love." Given Gioia's recurrent elegies to his late son, Michael Jasper, one can read this poem as an apostrophe to him (line 3, after all, refers to "blood-soaked jasper"). But the poem allows the reader to imagine any lost beloved since this elegy's appeal is as universal as the sea. The speaker watches the beach, its rocks, its shells, its gulls and cormorants, and he marvels "how time makes hardness shine." In unusually concrete, vivid images, Gioia conjures the physical world and how time and the natural world continuously remake it. He tells the dead beloved that the pebbles

> come in every color, pure or mixed,
> gray-green of basalt, blood-soaked jasper, quartz,
> granite and feldspar, even bits of glass,
> smoothed by the patient jeweller of the tides. (49)

From observing this process, Gioia infers the smallness of death, but nature fails to console since "A falcon watches from the ridge, indifferent / to the burdens" he has brought to the shore. "Sea Pebbles" then ends with heartrending closure, the speaker "hollow as driftwood, dead as any stone" (49). The poem closes by knitting key images and diction from its setting into its figurative language that manifests ongoing grief: "No point in walking farther, so I sit, / hollow as driftwood, dead as any stone" (49). In these final two lines, the alliteration of *d* sounds and the unvarying iambic blank verse— except for the initial trochee in the last line that underscores how "*Ho*llow" the speaker feels—suggest a relentlessness like that of the sea and its tides.

"Vultures Mating" similarly evokes the sensuousness of nature in adroit free verse structured in five-line stanzas. Perched on "a large dead tree" and "ripe with the perfume of her fertility" and "stinking of carrion," a female vulture attracts a flock of wooing males who hold "their red scabrous heads erect." This mixture of death and desire widens to encompass "the world":

> The stink and splendor of fertility
> arouses the world. The rotting log
> flowers with green moss. The fallen chestnut
> splits and drives its root into the soil.
> The golden air pours down its pollen. (50)

Here, unlike in the personal perspective of "Sea Pebbles," the objective point of view uncovers a natural inextricability of death and life that affords some solace and embodies an overflowing ripeness through alliteration of the *b* sound in its terminal lines: "each damp and fecund *b*ud yearning to *b*urst, / to *b*urn, to *b*lossom, to *b*egin" (50). To serve their subjects well, in both this poem and "Sea Pebbles," Gioia effectively relies on imagery that goes beyond his stated aesthetic in "The Next Poem" of presenting only "those few unshakeable details / that no confusion can erase."

"My Handsome Cousin" and "Style" also dance with death but in distinct ways. Like "Finding a Box of Family Letters," "My Handsome Cousin" approaches death in a fanciful way. Whereas in the heartfelt "Finding a Box" Gioia responds to a photo of his dead parents at a banquet and urges them facetiously to get on the dance floor, in "My Handsome Cousin" he converses with the dead through a dream. In tercets of free-verse lines often iambic, the surreal poem opens with the dead cousin declaring that he's not really dead but has "'been away.'" He then says he has come back to show the speaker the house he lives in. The speaker thinks of the dead man's gray widow and grown children who know their father "from old photographs." Clearly confused and skeptical, he wants to ask his cousin where he'd been. But the cousin gets the last, surprising word, announcing, "'It's time to go next door. / Let's see the house that will be yours'" (73). With this ending, Gioia generates a *frisson* for the reader that recalls the experience of reading his ghost story, "Haunted." Gioia has said that "A successful poem first entices the reader to enter an imaginary space and then creates the urgency to collaborate with the author in completing it" (Johnson 29). "My Handsome Cousin" does just this, leading the reader to realize that if "it's time to go next door" to the house the speaker soon will inhabit, it's time for him to face his death.

In "Style," Gioia confronts death by skillfully telling the story through a narrator as witness. Charlie functions much like Nick Carraway in *The Great Gatsby*, a less worldly and polished man easily impressed by his successful, elegant friend but also fated both to find in him the dark side of humanity and to bear witness to it. Charlie opens the six-section, blank-verse monologue by idolizing his friend Tom's Cary Grant perfection in clothes and conduct. Charlie then reads our minds. He baldly states what he knows readers think: "My story and my friend seem superficial" (140). In fact, his own style lacks sophistication, which Gioia reinforces through Charlie's brief simple sentences and frequent end-stopped lines:

> What does style matter? Quite a lot, I say.
> Style isn't fashion. It's knowing who you are
> And how you hold yourself up to the world.
> It's the clear surface that lets you see the depths. (140-41)

So, Charlie keeps us listening, waiting to find out who Tom really is.

Gioia gins the suspense by having Charlie ask, in the midst of envying the appurtenances of Tom's lavish lifestyle, "Who could have guessed the way the story ended?" (142). Charlie soon learns from Tom's wife, Eden, that a mysterious illness has left Tom "no longer" looking "at all like Tom":

> His face kept getting worse. One afternoon
> When I came home from work, he left the room.
> Shutting the door, he cried, "Don't look at me!"
> I leaned against the door and said I loved him
> No matter what he looked like. I see now
> What a mistake that was. Later that night
> He took the mirrors down in the apartment. (145)

By having Tom take "the mirrors down" before decamping alone to a sordid walk-up, Gioia presents a symbol of Tom's lost identity. Behind his door, Tom becomes just "a voice" (146). At Eden's request, Charlie, who thinks he's "just a human blur" compared to stylish Tom (140), goes to face his friend and what he represents. Here, in the plot's climax, Charlie finds Tom holed up in his tenement like the permanently transformed Henry Jekyll in his cabinet, awaiting self-destruction by his own monstrous second self.

Gioia's plotting answers our suspense about Tom, but it also leaves us questioning the narrator Charlie's love of style. In the climactic scene, Charlie vividly describes the monster he "did not recognize," a being who has learned in an almost-empty room that "Reality" has "no style" (147, 149). So Charlie sees Tom naked without his stylish persona, and what's left is monstrous and hollow, having "no style" at all. The meeting dramatically ends in nihilistic violence that Gioia renders concretely in quick, short sentences enlivened by internal rhyme, a pair of spondees, and alliteration of the *f* sound:

> He took a book of matches from his pocket.
> Struck one. It flamed. He dropped it on the floor.
> The fuel-soaked papers at his feet took fire.
> "You'd better go," he said. I backed away.
> The inferno had been carefully devised.
> The blaze reached out in lines across the room.
> As the fire spread, the flames were beautiful. (149)

Just as Mr. Hyde destroys Henry Jekyll, Tom's dark double proves self-consuming.

But does Charlie learn from what he has witnessed? That he finds the flames of Tom's self-immolation "beautiful" and not horrific may well make him an unreliable narrator. Like Nick in *The Great Gatsby* or Gabriel Utterson in *Dr. Jekyll and Mr. Hyde*, Charlie serves as a reader-identification figure, but by the end of "Style," readers need to rely on their own devices to interpret the story. Gioia concludes the last section by letting Charlie take control of Tom's self-styled "denouement"; he visits Tom's wife, whom he regards as "perfect" and "beautiful" (142), and Charlie kindly but self-servingly invents Tom's final words of compassion to her. Blind to the warning of Tom's cautionary tale, Charlie literally takes Tom's stylish place as he and Eden talk "on an immaculate divan / Beneath a David Hockney Swimming Pool" (150). At the beginning, Charlie tells us style is the "surface that lets you see the depths" (141), but the depths that Tom sees contain his empty and hellish inner reality, and he has his epiphany only once he's lost all style. Like the murderer in "Homecoming," Tom as monster chooses evil. In contrast, Charlie's ongoing pursuit of style suggests he has not yet recognized his monster within. "Style," then, is a well-crafted, suspenseful psychological tale delivered by a narrator we learn to distrust.

Because *99 Poems* encapsulates Gioia's entire career, assessing it is tantamount to figuring his place in contemporary poetry. Randall Jarrell famously writes in his "Reflections on Wallace Stevens," "A good poet is someone who manages, in a lifetime of standing out in thunderstorms, to be struck by lightning five or six times; a dozen or two dozen times and he is great" (148). It is easy to list a handful of poems in this book that meet this measure. "Planting a Sequoia," "California Hills in August," "In Cheever Country," "Special Treatments Ward," "Words," "Sea Pebbles: An Elegy," "Equations of the Light," "The Lost Garden," "Prayer," "Shopping," "Marriage of Many Years," "The Voyeur," "The Next Poem," and "All Souls'" all might qualify. And then there are the widely recognized narratives to consider, such as "Counting the Children," "The Homecoming," and "Haunted." Even allowing for vagaries of taste, it's clear from the best work in *99 Poems* that Gioia has many times, as he puts it in "Prayer," come close to a "blade of lightning / harvesting the sky."

THE BALLAD OF JESÚS ORTIZ (2018)

With *The Ballad of Jesús Ortiz*, Gioia engaged with cowboy poetry for the first time. In "Disappearing Ink," Gioia identified cowboy poetry as one branch of popular verse revitalizing American poetry through oral performance (7). Barney Nelson has rebutted Gioia's claim by arguing that "Cowboy poetry has always been written down" and that "many of the 'anonymous' poems recited at the early gatherings [of cowboy poetry such as at Elko, Nevada, in 1985] have since been traced to published authors" (404). The Western Folklife Center, which organized the Elko gathering, also underscores that cowboy poetry is "written." Yet Edward Hirsch clarifies that in addition "there is a strong oral and storytelling component to cowboy poetry," as well as "a decided emphasis on performance" (138), which supports Gioia's characterization. Nevertheless, the center's definition would disqualify Gioia's poem in this subgenre since the center maintains that the verse is "written by someone who has lived a significant portion of his or her life in the Western North American cattle culture" (qtd. in Hirsch 138). Still, this requirement is flexible, for as David Stanley explains, "ranching people have also embraced verse by non-cowboys" with no firsthand knowledge of "livestock and cattle management" (6-7). Gioia's ballad about cowboys in the Old West came to him secondhand from his grandfather, a second-generation vaquero, but his story is authentic, and according to Stanley's criteria, Gioia's cowboy poem is too. In fact, the Wyoming state librarian supplied Gioia with newspaper articles documenting the grandfather's tale (Zheng 89-90). So, *The Ballad of Jesús Ortiz* is a cowboy ballad remembering a true story of life in the Old West in written rhymed quatrains meant to be read or recited aloud, as Gioia has done for the BBC (Zheng 92-93).

The germ of Gioia's ballad is the stuff of an oral tradition that flourished in the vaqueros' work camps, as Cynthia L. Vidaurri has found (262). In describing the poem's genesis, Gioia relates that when he was ten, his Mexican grandfather told the boy that he had quit going to school around ten years old to become a cowboy. Gioia explains, "I asked him why he had left. 'My dad got shot in a saloon,' he replied. 'My brother and I had to support the family so we became cowboys.'" Gioia's grandfather "then described his father's death and his early days on the Wyoming frontier as a *vaquero*" (Zheng 88–89). In his author's note to the poem, Gioia offers that his ballad "describes the life and death of my great-grandfather. Every name, place, and significant event is true," and his poem records "the stories of the poor" from "the Old West."

The 116-line narrative opens with Jesús, or Jake, riding on the range with his father, herding to market "three thousand head of cattle." After "ten years on the open range," Jake gives up "the vaquero's life" and heads to Wyoming, where he settles in the town Lost Cabin and gets hired to tend John Okie's bar. The turning point comes one night when Jake cuts off a drunk with an unpaid tab. Bill Howard leaves in a huff but returns with a rifle and brutally kills the "'piss-poor Mexican peon.'" A posse finds Howard, and then "there were two more graves in Wyoming." The poem ends as two boys, one of them Gioia's grandfather, head off on a cattle drive. This plot about Jesús closely fits the genre of *tragedia corridos*, which are sung Mexican folk-ballad tragedies. Vidaurri explains that they "documented unfortunate events that happened to usually innocent individuals, making the stories all the more tragic" (262).

Gioia tells this story in ballad stanzas. Since "the people remembered in the poem sang and recited ballads," he decided that "the form seemed the right way to tell their story," according to the author's note. He also strove to make the music of his lines suggest the sung ballad (Zheng 91). It is of course the most common form of cowboy verse, inherited from the written ballads of eighteenth-century Britain. These ballads typically employed common meter, with four accents in lines 1 and 3 and three accents in lines 2 and 4, which would also rhyme. In *The Ballad of Jesús Ortiz*, Gioia establishes a metrical norm of three beats per line and, as expected, rhymes lines 2 and 4 of each stanza. The opening quatrain sets the pattern:

> Jake's *family* were va*que*ros.
> They *worked* the *cattle drives*
> *Down* from Mon*tana* to *market*.
> They *did* what it *took* to sur*vive*.

For variety and for emphasis, Gioia varies the meter. Here, all his lines contain three beats, but the first two lines scan as accentual-syllabic (iambic trimeter), whereas the next pair is accentual (three beats per line, or half meter). Later, while describing Okie's monopoly in Lost Cabin, the meter thickens in line 3 to four accents and repeats the verb *owned* to approximate Okie's wide holdings:

> John Okie owned the town,
> The Sheep King of Wyoming.
> He *owned* the *herds*. He *owned* the *land*
> And every wild thing roaming.

This quatrain's consistent accentual-syllabic pattern—all lines are iambic—further helps the longer third line stand out with its extra stressed syllable.

Besides meter, Gioia exploits form through rhyme, syntax, and sounds. For instance, he varies his types of rhymes. While most are true rhymes of one syllable, such as "tar" and "bar," in the passage above we see him using double rhyme with "W*yoming*" and "*roaming*." In the next stanza the double rhyme is slightly awry as the language becomes aptly colloquial:

> He let him sleep in the kitchen.
> Mexicans worked hard
> And didn't waste time bitching.

Gioia enriches the simple form in other ways, too, including syntactic repetition of the phrase "three thousand head of cattle":

Three thousand head of cattle
Grazing the prairie grass,
Three thousand head of cattle
Pushed through each mountain pass.

Three thousand head of cattle
Fording the muddy streams,
And then three thousand phantoms
Bellowing in your dreams.

So he repeats the phrase three times only to vary it tellingly the fourth time, when sleep turns the cattle to "phantoms." He also employs alliteration and consonance, as in the closing lines of the poem: "With hardly a *w*ord for their mother / Who *w*atched them ride a*w*ay." So, the inherited story, the plotting, and the ballad stanza all work to form an entertaining tale that documents life in the Old West. With this cowboy ballad, Gioia justifies the label western writer as it's traditionally applied while recording family history.

Chapter 4

THE POET AS CRITIC AND PUBLIC INTELLECTUAL

Dana Gioia is a poet who writes criticism seriously and who undertakes editing projects that serve poetry's greater cause. This role of public intellectual was filled in Auden and Eliot's time by the quaint "man of letters." Not all freelance writers qualify as public intellectuals, however. In evaluating the career of Alfred Kazin, Thomas Bender distinguishes the public intellectual not just by the writer's status as nonspecialist but also by the uses of literature. Kazin "used literature for larger purposes, to talk about subjects that mattered to contemporary society. His capacity to speak to more general and deeply felt worries, questions and aspirations, and to do so in a common idiom, made him a public intellectual" (qtd. in Garber 20).

This characterization of Kazin goes far in describing what Gioia does and why. Gioia told John Cusatis that as a graduate student he loved to read essays by Wendell Berry, Donald Hall, and Cynthia Ozick, "public intellectuals writing for a broad but mixed audience. I knew early that they were my people" (332). After Gioia left his job as a vice president at General Foods, he turned to writing for his livelihood. Gioia eventually left New York at age forty-five for his native California, where he forged ahead as a professional "man of letters"—not a university specialist in creative writing. Though a decade lapsed between his second and third books of poems and another eleven years between the third and the fourth, Gioia has never swerved from his primary identity as poet. In fact, everything Gioia does simultaneously serves the cause of his own poetry and his quest for poetry to reach a wider audience of educated but nonspecialized readers. As a result, he was a natural fit for the National Endowment for the Arts.

As a public intellectual, Gioia's most deeply felt worry is the divorce of poetry from the educated general reader and the resulting isolation of poets from a common audience. In 1991, in "Can Poetry Matter?," he amplified the problem like this:

> The most serious question for the future of American culture is whether the arts will continue to exist in isolation and decline into subsidized academic specialties or whether some possibility of rapprochement with the educated public remains. . . . Given the decline of literacy, the proliferation of other media, the crisis in humanities education, the collapse of critical standards, and the sheer weight of past failures, how can poets possibly succeed in being heard? (18)

Here Gioia expresses his greatest wish: "that poetry could again become a part of American public culture" (19). Poetry, he feels, must recruit its readership from the people who in general support the arts, the well-educated people who cut across occupational boundaries but who commonly attend performances of symphonies and operas and screenings of foreign films, who buy jazz and classical music, who read literary fiction and biography, who listen to National Public Radio ("Can" 16). Gioia wants our culture to meet Walt Whitman's challenge that " 'To have great poets, there must be great audiences, too' " ("Can" 10).

Through his essays in the eighties, Gioia established the defense of New Formalism in much the same way that Wordsworth's preface to *Lyrical Ballads* paved the way for Romanticism in 1800. Wordsworth conditioned his audience to accept the turn in literary history that his works embody. In other words, he exploited the preface as a marketing tool; its earliest incarnation in the first edition of 1798 was labeled an "Advertisement." Similarly, in "Notes on the New Formalism" and "The Poet in the Age of Prose"—both reprinted in *Can Poetry Matter?*—Gioia argues for a revival of form in poetry to parallel the return to tonality in music, representation in art, and ornamental detail in architecture ("Notes" 36). These shifts resemble the New Formalists' reactions against free verse, which once aided an earlier poetic revolution but now serves the old-guard establishment. Poets reviving formal verse, like painters returning from abstraction to realism, represent the fresh "unexpected challenge," Gioia says, which gives them appeal to audiences, as do their means ("Notes" 29). In "The Poet in the Age of Prose," Gioia establishes that from the beginning the New Formalists made reaching an audience primary to their mission:

> New Formalism represents the latest in this series of rebellions against poetry's cultural marginality. The generational change in literary sensibility, which would eventually be called New Formalism, began . . . when a group of young writers created—admittedly, only in their own minds—a new audience for poetry. Alienated from the kind of verse being praised and promulgated in the university, these young poets—like every new generation of writers—sought to define their own emerging art in relation to an imaginary audience. (224)

The purpose of reviving form and meter, he argues, is to widen the audience for poetry and to provide poets with long-dormant possibilities for fresh expression.

Gioia revives this concern for audience in "Disappearing Ink: Poetry at the End of Print Culture," the lead essay of his third critical collection. It speculates on the directions of poetry within American culture in the twenty-first century. In an age when print competes with technology and mass media, Gioia observes that the major change in the world of poetry is the rise of popular poetry—

rap, cowboy verse, spoken word, performance poetry, and poetry slams. Gioia, whose essay is analytical and not evaluative, nevertheless allows that "most of this verse is undistinguished or worse" (7). But what matters is that all these types of poetry are oral and all draw audiences "hungry for what poetry provides" (19). Despite the challenges to print poetry and to the literary dominance of universities, the changes in literary poetry toward rhyme and meter locate it within the cultural "shift in sensibility toward orality" more obviously seen in rap or cowboy verse (29). As a result, Gioia concludes, "For the first time in a century there is the possibility of serious literary poetry reengaging a nonspecialized audience of artists and intellectuals, both in and out of the academy" (31). Ironically, much of this reengagement occurs during oral readings at bookstores—though, like ink, they're disappearing, too.

A prime goal of Gioia's at the NEA was to reverse the decline in reading, a cultural problem fully explored in the agency's 2004 report *Reading at Risk: A Survey of Literary Reading in America*. As a partial remedy, Gioia launched The Big Read, which through grants, discussion guides, and compact discs has encouraged residents of cities and towns to read and talk about a single work within their community. Choices originally included F. Scott Fitzgerald's *The Great Gatsby*, Ray Bradbury's *Fahrenheit 451*, Harper Lee's *To Kill a Mockingbird*, and Zora Neale Hurston's *Their Eyes Were Watching God*. Gioia's mission to boost reading derives from his belief that literary works fulfill the human "need for stories" that deepen "the meaning of our own lives," as he explains in a preface to a coedited textbook (Kennedy 15). His stint teaching at the University of Southern California clearly supported this longtime effort to boost reading, in this case the reading of poetry among undergraduates. As he told Father Sean Salai, who interviewed him for *America*, his course enrolled up to two hundred students whom he challenged not only by assigning papers and exams but also by making them recite poems they have memorized, all to emphasize the experiential approach to poems that can enchant readers ("Catholic Poet").

Naturally, his textbook of choice was the one he coedited with X. J. Kennedy, *An Introduction to Poetry*.

Another key way to meet the challenge of creating readers, especially audiences for poetry, is to produce better anthologies, for these volumes "are poetry's gateway to the general culture" ("Can" 20). Among Gioia's books are fifteen textbooks and anthologies, including the two just mentioned. All of these texts are the kinds of books that not only serve the demands of the classroom but also just might remain in the private libraries of money-strapped students. Gioia longs for the days when poetry anthologies by the likes of Oscar Williams and Louis Untermeyer sold in huge quantities to general readers and consistently updated the best of contemporary writing. In *An Introduction to Poetry*, he and poet X. J. Kennedy demonstrate how college textbooks can fill the same role. Gioia's chief criterion for anthologies is that they present "masterpieces, not mediocrity" ("Can" 20), and this collection meets the requirement consistently. But among its hundreds of poems, Gioia and Kennedy include not just warhorses but also samples from many up-and-coming poets.

This last distinction of his anthology points to the role his criticism has played in bringing notice to unfairly neglected poets. The poet who spent years plying his craft at night and holding his poems from circulation repeatedly focuses on previously neglected writers. His own years of loneliness as a writer primed Gioia to understand, as he puts it elsewhere, that "the contemporary poet has reluctantly learned to expect obscurity and isolation—not only from readers but from other artists—as conditions inseparable from his craft" ("Afterword" 19). For example, *Studying with Miss Bishop* devotes a chapter to Ronald Perry, an all-but-forgotten poet who resided in Nassau and died in middle age, and large parts of *Can Poetry Matter?* cast light on previously overshadowed poets such as Jared Carter, Tom Disch, Weldon Kees, and Ted Kooser. Gioia writes with convincing, sympathetic intelligence about all of them. Just as he has worked to broaden the audience for poetry in general, so here he works to gain an audience for neglected talent. Through his appraisals of the noncanonical, then, Gioia teaches "remedial reading," as David Mason puts it ("Inner" 143).

The other three collections of essays similarly strive to bring notice to poets who deserve to be better known. *Barrier of a Common Language: An American Looks at Contemporary British Poetry* advocates for Ted Hughes and Philip Larkin, whose slots in the canon are secure, as well as for Charles Causley, Tony Connor, and Dick Davis, who are less likely to land on Americans' reading lists. *Disappearing Ink* promotes the poetry of Samuel Menashe, Kenneth Rexroth, and Kay Ryan, who subsequently became Poet Laureate. Moreover, in "Longfellow in the Aftermath of Modernism," Gioia takes on the task of rehabilitating the reputation of Henry Wadsworth Longfellow, once the most famous American poet in the world but now nearly eradicated from anthologies and represented by only a handful of lyric poems and short excerpts from narratives. Gioia accounts for this seismic change and argues that Longfellow's work, including his accomplishments in narrative and in prosody, need to be reevaluated not by the values of modernism but by those of his own time, the nineteenth century. Gioia keeps his eyes open to Longfellow's deficiencies, including the lack of tragic vision, but considers his place in American literature safe: "You will have to go a long way round if you want to ignore him" ("Longfellow" 86). Finally, in separate essays, *The Catholic Writer Today* promotes the almost-forgotten poets Brother Antoninus, Elizabeth Jennings, and Dunstan Thompson. Thompson's "early work has been out of print for seventy years" ("Two Poets" 77). The reputation of Brother Antoninus has fallen in the last quarter century since he died, and his "legacy" is "still too little known, even by Catholics" ("Brother" 100, 107). And Jennings, whose poetic life "began splendidly," saw her luck run out and her career stall as her inclusion in The Movement led to "a dead end" ("Clarify" 108). In his essays on these three Catholic writers, Gioia recovers their lost reputations.

Besides promoting good poems and neglected talent in his anthologies, as editor of *The Best American Poetry: 2018*, Gioia has shined attention on poetry's contemporary variety as well as its quality, a sure way to widen its appeal. Poetry, it would seem, no longer is trapped in dire straits. Making his selections from more than five thousand poems, Gioia discovered that poetry still matters and in more ways than ever. But the old culture wars that pitted free verse against formal verse now seem quaint, if remembered at all. "Anything goes," Gioia found:

> A benevolent sanity prevails in which poets seem free to write in whatever way inspiration suggests. I was pleased to see individual writers publish work in widely different styles, sometimes even in the same issue of a journal. Free verse remains the dominant mode, but rhyme and meter are widely used again, often in ways that imitate hip-hop. Prose poems still make a strong showing. . . . It was a pleasure to turn the pages of a journal and not know what to expect next. (Introduction xxx–xxxi)

So, there is no mainstream anymore, only a gamut of alternatives, which includes forms of performance he could not reproduce in the print anthology. Above all, Gioia's selections mirror "the social complexity" of America and "poetry's regional variety." He learned "there are fine writers everywhere" (xxix–xxx). No wonder the audience for poetry is "rapidly growing," he concluded (xxiii).

Gioia's poetic versatility and his cause for poetry in general—the need to entertain, to find a broader audience, to find ways to merge low and high culture as well as to combine poetry and the other arts—are vividly embodied not only by his anthologies and his essays written for the common reader but also by his four libretti. His first, *Nosferatu: An Opera Libretto*, was written for composer Alva Henderson and published in 2001 as a book. Gioia based it on F. W. Murnau's great silent film of 1922, an adaptation of Bram Stoker's gothic novel *Dracula*. In Murnau's film, Gioia found a Romantic myth natural to opera. In an informative essay that Gioia appends to the libretto, "*Sotto Voce*," he comments that with each scene he first wrote the lyrics to the central aria and then wrote the parts that preceded and followed it (*Nosferatu* 83). He generated ten arias that provide the plot's emotional peaks. Among the best are the three arias that also appear in *Interrogations*: "Ellen's Dream," "Eric's Mad Song," and "Nosferatu's Nocturne" ("Nosferatu's Serenade" in *Interrogations at Noon*). These lyrics vary their rhyme schemes and meters, but all the verse is clear, direct, and musical. The second libretto was written for composer Paul Salerni's *Tony Caruso's Final Broadcast* (published in 2005 in *Italian Americana*). Gioia creates ten short scenes centering on Caruso's last show, "Opera Lover," and probes Tony's failed dream to become the "second Caruso." *Pity the Beautiful* excerpts four of the songs, including "Maria Callas's Aria," which is sung by the ghost of Maria Callas, who pays Tony a visit. Gioia's other two libretti are *The Three Feathers* for Lori Laitman (premiered 2014) and *Haunted* for Salerni (premiered 2019). In a sense, Gioia's own orality includes performance and recordings of these operas. Other works have been set to music by such composers as Morten Lauridsen, Ned Rorem, and Dave Brubeck. As librettist, Gioia extends the literary diversity that distinguishes his work. Like Auden, who wrote libretti and critical essays as well as poetry, Gioia has also published libretti and essays as well as translations. As with Auden, however, with Gioia what matters most is his own poetry.

Chapter 5

THE POET AS CATHOLIC WRITER

As he has aged, Dana Gioia has come to recognize that the essence of his identity lies in his Catholic faith. "For years," he told Father Salai, "I didn't think of myself as a Catholic poet—just as a writer who was a Catholic" ("Catholic Poet"). He avoided Mass for twenty years until in middle age he returned to the communion rail ("Singing" 212). Though his early poems were written without this conscious awareness of the Catholic worldview, sometimes, as in "Daily Horoscope" and "In Cheever Country," he addressed his spiritual hunger and evoked a visionary realism or sacramental reality. Increasingly, though, he realized that "Catholicism is in my DNA," as he puts it, and that "every poem I have ever written reflects my Catholic worldview" (Snyder 153). At times in his work religion became overt. For instance, his first two libretti, *Nosferatu* and *Tony Caruso's Final Broadcast*, draw explicitly on elements of Catholicism, incorporating the *Salve Regina* and *Tantum Ergo*. And several poems in *Interrogations at Noon* and *Pity the Beautiful* address religious subjects directly. But what makes a writer Catholic is not so much the subject matter as the incorporation of other spiritual aspects: sacramental nature, the long view, redemption through suffering, and the "continuity between the living and the dead" ("Catholic Writer" 20).

Unsurprisingly, then, Gioia's poetry has drawn scholarly attention for its Catholic sensibility. Notably, for an edited collection of essays on contemporary Catholic poetry, Gary M. Bouchard analyzes the "Catholic vision" in poems from *Interrogations at Noon* and compares Gioia to two other contemporary poets (137), whereas in an article for the journal *Renascence,* Janet McCann has focused on Gioia's metaphysics and links him to Graham Greene, another Catholic writer who portrays how grace can redeem the damned (201). Most recently, in his essay *The Catholic Imagination in Modern American Poetry,* James Matthew Wilson places Gioia with Frederick Turner and Paul Mariani as poets who "perpetuate the Catholic imagination as sacramental and universal." In poems such as "Haunted," Wilson finds, Gioia represents "the experience of being haunted by God's presence and our bottomless desire for salvation" (30, 33). In contrast, Roxana Elena Doncu contends that while "there is a metaphysical/Catholic dimension to his poetry," Gioia is not really "a Catholic or religious poet" (12).

Although Bouchard, McCann, and Wilson all find a common Catholic vision in Gioia and other writers, a chief contention of "The Catholic Writer Today" is that contemporary Catholic writers are isolated and scattered and have no current tradition to sustain them. Not only is there no Catholic tradition in mainstream America, but also the Church itself lacks interest in the arts. Gioia asserts that "the Church has lost its imagination and creativity" ("Catholic Writer" 33), pointing to "the graceless architecture" of its newly erected buildings and its "poorly performed music" ("Catholic Writer" 38). Gioia quips, "I deserve to suffer for my sins, but must so much of that punishment take place in church?" Forgotten is the "great strength" of the Church: "its glorious physicality, its ability to convey its truths as incarnate" through the beauty of music, architecture, painting, and poetry ("Catholic Writer" 37-38).

Gioia's complaints encircle all the arts, but in "The Catholic Writer Today" he centers on literature and establishes the lack of current tradition by describing the rich community of Catholic writers that flourished from 1945 to 1965. He lists five dozen novelists, poets, and critics of Catholic identity who were well known in America and honored with sixteen Pulitzer Prizes and National Book Awards. To this esteemed group he adds more prominent names from the British Catholic Revival who attracted wide readership in America:

Anthony Burgess, Graham Greene, Muriel Spark, J. R. R. Tolkien, and Evelyn Waugh, among others. Catholic Irish writers such as Frank O'Connor and Flann O'Brien were also popular at this time. All these writers commonly expressed the Catholic worldview. Figures such as Thomas Merton, Flannery O'Connor, and Walker Percy formed a significant minority tributary to the American cultural mainstream. Today, however, American literature itself suffers diminishment. As Gioia contends, without a strong Catholic tradition, contemporary art suffers from a spiritual void, having lost the "transcendent religious vision" that had nurtured artists and their audiences for two thousand years ("Catholic Writer" 35).

Nevertheless, Gioia ends his essay with hope. He believes that the hunger for beauty and art in a Church that thinks "Catholicism and art no longer mix" can yet be fed and that a literary tradition can be renewed ("Catholic Writer" 18). But the renewal won't come from within the Church and its clergy, Gioia asserts; instead, the renewal will be led by the disconnected writers themselves, just as a few like-minded but scattered poets founded the Romantic Movement upon the ashes of a moribund neoclassical tradition. The Catholic writers enjoy the advantage of a rock to build upon, a worldview embodied by centuries of art and a tradition of symbols that puts the Catholic poet and novelist "at the center of the Western tradition" ("Catholic Writer" 41). Aware of this foundation, in 2015, Gioia inaugurated the biannual Catholic Imagination Conference, aiming to foster a community of Catholic writers that might begin to emulate the literary culture of postwar America. Nothing happens overnight, but in 2019, at the third conference held at Loyola University in Chicago, attendance reached nearly five hundred (Mastromatteo).

Besides starting the conference, Gioia has attempted to re-create a Catholic literary culture by writing about earlier poets who represent models to contemporary Catholic writers. In *The Catholic Writer Today* he centers on the metaphysical poet John Donne, Jesuit priest Gerard Manley Hopkins, the Beat poet Brother Antoninus, Dunstan Thompson, who was gay as well as Catholic, and British poet Elizabeth

Jennings. Through both her use of traditional meter and rhyme and her expression of a Catholic worldview and sacramentalism, Jennings seems to have particularly influenced Gioia the poet. Although all these poets belong to previous generations, their examples, like Dante's, show current Catholic poets how to rewrite the central Catholic theme of the difficult spiritual journey to redemption and how to unveil the invisible world incarnated in the world of the senses ("Catholic Writer" 42). Consistent with his earlier appraisals of overlooked poets such as Dick Davis, Kay Ryan, and Radcliffe Squires, Gioia's focus on Brother Antoninus, Jennings, and Thompson shines light on poets fallen into shadows. Even his criticism manifests redemption.

Most of *The Catholic Writer Today* concerns the relations of literature and faith, but in its third section, Gioia more broadly performs his role as a Catholic public intellectual while maintaining connections to the title essay's ideas. For example, the theme of the redemptive nature of suffering informs his thinking about Paul's letter to the Philippians. Old and tired and facing possible execution, Paul abandons his typical mode of argument and abstraction, Gioia suggests. In its place, Paul adopts what Gioia calls a "simple human touch": Paul not only presents parts of his letter in verse, conveying through poetic beauty "Christ's incarnation and death" ("Epistle" 180, 189), but also makes this final letter a personal and intimate expression of his own pursuit of redemptive suffering. Gioia clearly identifies with this pursuit and has performed it poetically in works such as "Special Treatments Ward." The concluding essay, "Singing Aquinas in L.A.," similarly addresses the power of beauty to enrapture believers. Gioia remembers singing as a schoolboy the blissful words of Thomas Aquinas's hymn *Tantum Ergo*, which forms part of the rite of the Eucharist called the Benediction. As only art can do, Aquinas's beautiful song embodied for the boy what he was not yet ready to fathom intellectually, the mystery of the Eucharist ("Singing" 210-11). For Gioia the poet, this song's power of enchantment and mystery represents what he elsewhere calls "the great potential of Christian literature to depict the material world, the physical world of the senses, while also revealing behind it another invisible and eternal dimension" ("Catholic Writer" 42). Other pieces meditate on the paintings of George Tooker and the sculptures of Luis Tapia, which incarnate beauty and spirituality, too.

All these nonliterary essays show that Gioia's aim in creating a new Catholic poetic tradition serves not only American literature, but also the Church and its Catholic community. Renewing Catholic poetry will renew the Church, for Gioia contends that in reclaiming beauty—in its art and architecture, its music and literature—the Church will regain "its ability to reach souls in the modern world" ("Catholic Writer" 38). Perhaps it is not unlike Paul reaching the Philippians through the poetic beauty of his six-line hymn about Christ's Incarnation.

The influential literary career of Dana Gioia now spans four decades. Besides his status as a poet of distinction, he has written extensively about poetry. His critical essays comprise not only appraisals of numerous poets, including both many unjustly neglected poets such as Ronald Perry and some earlier figures such as Longfellow and Donne, but they also develop arguments about poetry's larger connections to American culture and solutions for making poetry more vital as a communal art and as a Catholic communal art. His extensive compiling of anthologies and textbooks, his work with the National Endowment for the Arts as the country's leading arts advocate, his service as the California State Poet Laureate, and his teaching at the University of Southern California—all these pursuits have pragmatically reinforced many ideas in his prose. Above all, as the key critic of the New Formalism and a Catholic literary renewal, the public intellectual has helped guide contemporary poets into new directions. This criticism on the revival of form and narrative and on the revival of Catholic poetic tradition applies most closely to his own poetry and thus embodies his poetics. Though diverse in subjects and styles, and even art forms when one considers his four libretti, Gioia's poetry shows little outwardly dramatic change in style from his first book to his most recent new and selected volume; there is, however, both a deepening of emotional power in his poetry, as late poems such as "Special Treatments Ward" and "Sea Pebbles: An Elegy" attest, and a more open expression of his Catholic spirituality and values, as in poems such as "Prayer at Winter Solstice" and "Marriage of Many Years." His verse has become more direct in expressing emotion while sustaining its artful craftsmanship—and thus has become all the more likely to endure. In the end, it is the combination of all of these achievements that makes Dana Gioia an important and compelling poet, critic, and public intellectual.

WORKS CITED

Baer, William. "An Interview with Dana Gioia." *The Formalist* 13.1 (2002): 18-49.

Barth, J. Robert, SJ. *The Symbolic Imagination.* 1977. Revised ed. New York: Fordham University Press, 2000.

Bate, Jonathan. *The Song of the Earth.* Cambridge, MA: Harvard University Press, 2001.

Bawer, Bruce. "The Flâneur, the Chemist, and the Chairman." *Hudson Review* 45.2 (2012): 333-39.

Bouchard, Gary M. "Our Litany: The Varied Voices and Common Vision of Three Contemporary Catholic Poets." In *Between Human and Divine: The Catholic Vision in Contemporary Literature,* edited by Mary R. Reichardt, 136-53. Washington, DC: Catholic University of America Press, 2010.

Brennan, Matthew. "Midlife Regret: Review of *Interrogations at Noon* by Dana Gioia." *American Book Review* (March–April 2002): 17.

Byers, Thomas B. "The Closing of the American Line: Expansive Poetry and Ideology." *Contemporary Literature* 33.2 (1992): 396-415.

Carnell, Simon. "Packaged Tours." *TLS,* December 27, 1991, 9.

Clark, Brooke. "Three Books." Review of *99 Poems: New & Selected. Able Muse* 22 (2016): 95-101.

Cusatis, John. "An Interview with Dana Gioia." In *Dictionary of Literary Biography: Twenty-First-Century American Poets, Third Series.* Vol. 380, edited by John Cusatis, 327-33. Farmington Hills, MI: Gale Cengage Learning, 2017.

Dawson, Ariel. "The Yuppie Poet." *AWP Newsletter,* May 1985.

Doncu, Roxana Elena. "Dana Gioia and the Dilemma of the New Poetry in the U.S." *Journal of Philology and Intercultural Communication* 3.2 (2019): 5-13.

Flamm, Matthew. "Yearning Disabled." *Village Voice,* August 19, 1986, 45.

Garber, Marjorie. *Academic Instincts.* Princeton, NJ: Princeton University Press, 2001.

Gioia, Dana. *Daily Horoscope.* St. Paul, MN: Graywolf Press, 1986.

———. "Symposium." *Crosscurrents* 8.2 (1989): 88-90.

———. *The Gods of Winter.* St. Paul, MN: Graywolf Press, 1991.

———. "Being Outted." *Witness* 10.2 (1996).

———. "Afterword: Creative Collaboration." In *Dana Gioia and Fine Press Printing: A Bibliographical Checklist,* compiled by Michael Peich, 19-31. New York: Kelly/Winterton Press, 2000.

————. *Interrogations at Noon.* St. Paul, MN: Graywolf Press, 2001.

————. *Nosferatu: An Opera Libretto.* St. Paul, MN: Graywolf Press, 2001.

————. *Can Poetry Matter? Essays on Poetry and American Culture.* Revised ed. Minneapolis: Graywolf Press, 2002. [Originally published 1992.]

————. "Can Poetry Matter?" In *Can Poetry Matter? Essays on Poetry and American Culture,* 1-24. Revised ed. Minneapolis: Graywolf Press, 2002.

————. "Notes on the New Formalism." In *Can Poetry Matter? Essays on Poetry and American Culture,* 31-45. Revised ed. Minneapolis: Graywolf Press, 2002.

————. "The Poet in an Age of Prose." In *Can Poetry Matter? Essays on Poetry and American Culture,* 31-45. Revised ed. Minneapolis: Graywolf Press, 2002.

————. "Tradition and an Individual Talent." In *Can Poetry Matter? Essays on Poetry and American Culture,* 31-45. Revised ed. Minneapolis: Graywolf Press, 2002.

————. *Barrier of a Common Language: Essays on Contemporary British Poetry.* Ann Arbor: University of Michigan Press, 2003.

————. *Disappearing Ink: Poetry at the End of Print Culture.* St. Paul, MN: Graywolf Press, 2004.

————. "Disappearing Ink: Poetry at the End of Print Culture." In *Disappearing Ink: Poetry at the End of Print Culture,* 3-31. St. Paul, MN: Graywolf Press, 2004.

————. "The Hand of the Poet: The Magical Value of Manuscripts." In *Disappearing Ink: Poetry at the End of Print Culture,* 33-52. St. Paul, MN: Graywolf Press, 2004.

————. "Longfellow in the Aftermath of Modernism." In *Disappearing Ink: Poetry at the End of Print Culture,* 53-86. St. Paul, MN: Graywolf Press, 2004.

————. "Tony Caruso's Final Broadcast." *Italian Americana* 23.1 (2005): 5-38.

————. "Literary L.A., with No Apology." *Los Angeles Times,* May 7, 2006.

————. *Lonely Impulse of Delight: One Reader's Childhood.* Mountain View, CA: Artichoke Editions, 2007.

————. *Pity the Beautiful.* Minneapolis: Graywolf Press, 2012.

————. *99 Poems: New & Selected.* Minneapolis: Graywolf Press, 2016.

————. *Poetry as Enchantment.* Belmont, NC: Wiseblood Books, 2016.

————. *The Ballad of Jesús Ortiz.* Ojai, CA: Providence Press, 2018.

————. "Introduction." In *The Best American Poetry: 2018,* edited by Dana Gioia, xxiii–xxxii. New York: Scribner Poetry, 2018.

————. *The Catholic Writer Today: And Other Essays.* Belmont, NC: Wiseblood Books, 2019.

————. "Brother Beat Meets Mr. Everson." In *The Catholic Writer Today: And Other Essays,* 100-107. Belmont, NC: Wiseblood Books, 2019.

————. "The Catholic Writer Today." In *The Catholic Writer Today: And Other Essays,* 17-43. Belmont, NC: Wiseblood Books, 2019.

————. "Clarify Me, Please, God of the Galaxies: Elizabeth Jennings." In *The Catholic Writer Today: And Other Essays*, 108-20. Belmont, NC: Wiseblood Books, 2019.

————. "Singing Aquinas in L.A." In *The Catholic Writer Today: And Other Essays*, 209-13. Belmont, NC: Wiseblood Books, 2019.

————. "Two Poets Named Dunstan Thompson." In *The Catholic Writer Today: And Other Essays*, 77-99. Belmont, NC: Wiseblood Books, 2019.

————. *Studying with Miss Bishop: Memoirs from a Young Writer's Life*. Philadelphia: Paul Dry Books, forthcoming.

Hagstrom, Jack W. C., and Bill Morgan. *Dana Gioia: A Descriptive Bibliography with Critical Essays*. Jackson, MS: Parrish House, 2002.

Hirsch, Edward. *A Poet's Glossary*. Boston: Houghton Mifflin Harcourt, 2014.

Jarrell, Randall. "Reflections on Wallace Stevens." In *Poetry and the Age*, 133-48. Expanded ed. Gainesville: University Press of Florida, 2001. [Originally published 1953.]

Johnson, Michelle. "Poetic Collaborations: A Conversation with Dana Gioia." *World Literature Today* (Sept.–Oct. 2011): 26-35.

Juster, A. M. "The Case for Dana Gioia." *CRB Digital*, May 15, 2016.

Kennedy, X. J., Dana Gioia, and Nina Revoyr. *Literature for Life*. Boston: Pearson, 2012.

Koss, Erika. "*Image* Interview with Dana Gioia." In *The Catholic Writer Today: And Other Essays*, 154-76. Belmont, NC: Wiseblood Books, 2019.

Kuzma, Greg. "Dana Gioia and the Poetry of Money." *Northwest Review* 26.3 (1988): 111-21.

Lindner, April. *Dana Gioia*. Western Writers Series 143. Boise: Boise State University, 2000.

Maio, Samuel. "Dana Gioia's Dramatic Monologues." *The Formalist* 13.1 (2002): 63-72.

Mason, David. "Other Lives: On Shorter Narrative Poems." *Verse* 7.3 (1990): 16-21.

————. "The Inner Exile of Dana Gioia." *Sewanee Review* 123.1 (2015): 133-46.

Massamilla, Stephen. "The Achievement of Dana Gioia: *99 Poems: New & Selected*." *Italian Americana* 35.1 (2017): 75-78.

Mastromatteo, Mike. "Catholic Voice in Fiction and Fine Art Poised for New Relevance." *Crux: Taking the Catholic Pulse*, September 29, 2019.

McCann, Janet. "Dana Gioia: A Contemporary Metaphysics." *Renascence* 61.3 (2009): 193-205.

McPhillips, Robert. "Dana Gioia: An Interview." *Verse* 9.2 (1992): 9-27.

————. "Review of *The Gods of Winter*." *Verse* 9.2 (1992): 111-14.

————. *The New Formalism: A Critical Introduction*. Expanded ed. Cincinnati: Textos Books, 2005. [Originally published 2003.]

Monsour, Leslie. "O Dark, Dark, Dark, amid the Blaze of Noon: The Poetry of Dana Gioia." *Able Muse* (Winter 2002).

Mortensen, Arthur. "A Brief Look: *Interrogations at Noon* by Dana Gioia." *Expansive Poetry and Music Online.*

National Endowment for the Arts. *Reading at Risk: A Survey of Literary Reading in America.* Washington, DC: National Endowment for the Arts, 2004.

Nelson, Barney. "Dana Gioia Is Wrong about Cowboy Poetry." *Western American Literature* 40.4 (2006): 404-22.

O'Connor, Kevin T. "Review of *Pity the Beautiful: Poems.*" *Harvard Review Online*, November 18, 2013.

Peters, Robert. "Commuter Poetry: Dana Gioia's *Daily Horoscope.*" *Paintbrush* 14 (1987): 50-54.

Publishers Weekly. Review of *Interrogations at Noon* by Dana Gioia. *Publishers Weekly*, March 1, 2001.

Publishers Weekly. Review of *99 Poems: New & Selected* by Dana Gioia. *Publishers Weekly*, February 15, 2016.

Salai, Sean, SJ. "Catholic Poet Dana Gioia: Is Poetry Still a Spiritual Vocation?" *America*, May 6, 2019.

Snyder, Robert Lance. "If Any Fire Endures beyond Its Flame: A Conversation with Dana Gioia." In *The Catholic Writer Today: And Other Essays*, 123-53. Belmont, NC: Wiseblood Books, 2019.

Stanley, David. "Cowboy Poetry Then and Now." In *Cowboy Poets and Cowboy Poetry*, edited by David Stanley and Elaine Thatcher, 1-18. Urbana: University of Illinois Press, 1999.

Stefanile, Felix. "Poets of Emulation: Dana Gioia and Jay Parini." *VIA: Voices in Italian Americana* 1.1 (1990): 35-50.

Stevenson, Anne. "The Poetry of Dana Gioia: A Review of *The Gods of Winter.*" In *Between the Iceberg and the Ship: Selected Essays*, 156-58. Ann Arbor: University of Michigan Press, 1998.

Vendler, Helen. "Ardor and Artifice: The Mozartian Touch of a Master Poet." *New Yorker*, March 12, 2001, 101-4.

Vidaurri, Cynthia L. "Levantando Versos and Other Vaquero Voices: Oral Traditions of South Texas Mexican American Cowboys." In *Cowboy Poets and Cowboy Poetry*, edited by David Stanley and Elaine Thatcher, 261-72. Urbana: University of Illinois Press, 1999.

Wakoski, Diane. "The New Conservatism in American Poetry." *American Book Review* (May-June 1986): 3.

Walzer, Kevin. *The Ghost of Tradition: Expansive Poetry and Postmodernism.* Ashland, OR: Story Line Press, 1998.

Welford, Theresa Malphrus. *Transatlantic Connections: The Movement and New Formalism.* Pasadena, CA: Story Line Press, 2019.

Wilson, James Matthew. *The Catholic Imagination in Modern American Poetry.* Milwaukee: Wiseblood Books, 2014.

———. *The Fortunes of Poetry in an Age of Unmaking.* Oregon: Wiseblood Books, 2015.

———. "In Christ-Haunted California: Dana Gioia's *99 Poems.*" *Catholic World Report*, April 26, 2016.

Zheng, John. " 'This Poem Has Had a Strange Destiny': Interview with Dana Gioia about *The Ballad of Jesús Ortiz.*" *Journal of Ethnic American Literature* 9 (2019): 88-93.

SELECTED BIBLIOGRAPHY

POETRY

Daily Horoscope. St. Paul, MN: Graywolf Press, 1986.

The Gods of Winter. St. Paul, MN: Graywolf Press, 1991; York, UK: Peterloo Poets, 1991.

Interrogations at Noon. St. Paul, MN: Graywolf Press, 2001.

Pity the Beautiful. Minneapolis: Graywolf Press, 2012.

99 Poems: New & Selected. Minneapolis: Graywolf Press, 2016.

CRITICAL COLLECTIONS

Can Poetry Matter? Essays on Poetry and American Culture. St. Paul, MN: Graywolf Press, 1992. [Revised 10th anniversary ed., 2002.]

Barrier of a Common Language: Essays on Contemporary British Poetry. Ann Arbor: University of Michigan Press, 2003.

Disappearing Ink: Poetry at the End of Print Culture. St. Paul, MN: Graywolf Press, 2004.

The Catholic Writer Today: And Other Essays. Belmont, CA: Wiseblood Books, 2019.

Studying with Miss Bishop: Memoirs from a Young Writer's Life. Philadelphia: Paul Dry Books, forthcoming.

INTERVIEWS AND ESSAYS

The Catholic Writer Today. Milwaukee: Wiseblood Books, 2014.

Poetry as Enchantment. Belmont, NC: Wiseblood Books, 2016.

Zheng, John, ed. *Conversations with Dana Gioia.* Jackson: University of Mississippi Press, forthcoming.

TRANSLATIONS

Montale, Eugenio. *Mottetti: Poems of Love*. St. Paul, MN: Graywolf Press, 1990.

Seneca. *The Madness of Hercules (Hercules Furens)*. In *Seneca: The Tragedies*. Vol. 2, 43-104. Edited by David Slavitt. Baltimore: Johns Hopkins University Press, 1995.

OPERA LIBRETTI

Nosferatu. St. Paul, MN: Graywolf Press, 2001. [Recording: Albany Records, 2005.]

"Tony Caruso's Final Broadcast." *Italian Americana* 23.1 (2005): 5-38. [Recording: Naxos, 2010.]

The Three Feathers. [Published only in score form, 2014.]

Haunted. Premiere 2019. [Unpublished.]

ANTHOLOGIES EDITED / HANDBOOKS

Poems from Italy. Co-edited with William Jay Smith. St. Paul, MN: New Rivers Press, 1985.

New Italian Poets. Co-edited with Michael Palma. Brownsville, OR: Story Line Press, 1991.

The Longman Anthology of Short Fiction: Stories and Authors in Context. Co-edited with R. S. Gwynn. New York: Longman, 2001.

The Misread City: New Literary Los Angeles. Co-edited with Scott Timberg. Los Angeles: Red Hen Press, 2003.

California Poetry: From the Gold Rush to the Present. Co-edited with Chryss Yost and Jack Hicks. Berkeley: Heyday, 2004.

Twentieth-Century American Poetics: Poets on the Art of Poetry. Co-edited with David Mason and Meg Schoerke with D. C. Stone. New York: McGraw Hill, 2004.

Twentieth-Century American Poetry. Co-edited with David Mason and Meg Schoerke with D. C. Stone. New York: McGraw Hill, 2004.

100 Great Poets of the English Language. With Dan Stone. New York: Penguin Academics, 2005.

The Art of the Short Story. Co-edited with R. S. Gwynn. New York: Longman, 2006.

Handbook of Literary Terms: Literature, Language, Theory. 2nd ed. Co-edited with X. J. Kennedy and Mark Bauerlein. New York: Longman, 2009.

An Introduction to Fiction. 11th ed. Co-edited with X. J. Kennedy. New York: Longman, 2010.

An Introduction to Poetry. 13th ed. Co-edited with X. J. Kennedy. New York: Longman, 2010.

Literature for Life. Co-edited with X. J. Kennedy and Nina Revoyr. New York: Pearson, 2013.

The Best American Poetry: 2018. Series edited by David Lehman. New York: Scribner Poetry, 2018.

Literature: An Introduction to Fiction, Poetry, Drama, and Writing. 14th ed. Co-edited with X. J. Kennedy and Dan Stone. New York: Pearson, 2020.

OTHER EDITIONS

Weldon Kees: The Ceremony and Other Stories. Omaha, NE: Abattoir Editions, 1983.

Weldon Kees: The Ceremony and Other Stories. Expanded ed. Port Townsend, WA: Graywolf Press, 1984.

Formal Introductions: An Investigative Anthology. West Chester, PA: Aralia Press, 1994.

Certain Solitudes: Essays on the Poetry of Donald Justice. Co-edited with William Logan. Fayetteville: University of Arkansas Press, 1997.

Selected Short Stories of Weldon Kees. Lincoln: University of Nebraska Press, 2002.

This Man's Army: A War in Fifty-Odd Sonnets, by John Allan Wyeth. Co-edited with Matthew Bruccoli. Columbia: University of South Carolina Press, 2008.

Sacred and Profane Love: The Poetry of John Donne. McLean, VA: Trinity Forum, 2010.

God's Grandeur: The Poems of Gerard Manley Hopkins. McLean, VA: Trinity Forum, 2016.

Jack Foley's Unmanageable Masterpiece: California Literary Timeline 1940–2005. Co-edited with Peter Whitfield. Morgantown, WV: Monongahela Books, 2019.

FINE PRESS EDITIONS

Daily Horoscope. Iowa City: Windhover Press, 1982.

Two Poems. New York: Bowery Press, 1982.

Letter to the Bahamas. Omaha, NE: Abattoir Editions, 1983.

Summer. West Chester, PA: Aralia Press, 1983.

Journeys in Sunlight. Cottondale, AL: Ex Ophidia, 1986.

Two Poems/Due Poesie. Verona, Italy: Stamperia Ampersand, 1987.

Words for Music. Tuscaloosa: Parallel Editions, 1987.

Planting a Sequoia. West Chester, PA: Aralia Press, 1991.

Juno Plots Her Revenge. (Translation of Seneca.) West Chester, PA: Aralia Press, 1993.

The Litany. West Chester, PA: Aralia Press, 1999.

On Being a California Poet. Dallas: Southern Methodist University Library, 2003.

Lonely Impulse of Delight: One Reader's Childhood. Mountain View, CA: Artichoke Editions, 2007.

Homage to Valerio Magrelli. Verona, Italy: Stamperia Ampersand, 2009.

The Living and the Dead: Translations of Mario Luzi. West Chester, PA: Aralia Press, 2012.

Film Noir. West Chester, PA: Aralia Press, 2014.

The Ballad of Jesús Ortiz. Ojai, CA: Providence Press, 2018.

Two Epitaphs. West Chester, PA: Aralia Press, 2019.

VOLUMES IN TRANSLATION

La ce bun poezia? Două eseuri despre poezia şi cultura americană. Translated by Mirella Baltă and Gabriel Stănescu. Bucharest: Criterion, 1998.

Interrogations at Noon: Selected Poems and Essays. (Translated into Russian.) Edited by Nikolai Paltsev. Translated by Paltsev et al. Moscow: Rosspen, 2007.

La Escala Ardiente: Seguida Del Ensayo ¿Importa la Poesia? Translated by José Emilio Pacheco, Elsa Cross, Hernán Bravo Varela, Zulai Marcela Funetes, Jennifer Clement, and Víctor Manual Mendiola. Mexico City: Ediciones el Tucán de Virginia, 2010.

Planting a Sequoia and Other Poems. Translated into Greek by Kostas Zotopoulos. Athens: Society de Kata, 2019.

La oscuridad intacta: Poemas escogidos. Translated into Spanish by Gustavo Solonzaro-Alfaro. Valencia, Spain: Editorial Pre-Textos, 2020.

KEY GOVERNMENT REPORTS

Reading at Risk: A Survey of Literary Reading in America. Washington, DC: National Endowment for the Arts, 2004.

How the United States Funds the Arts. 2nd ed. With Tyler Cowen. Washington, DC: National Endowment for the Arts, 2007. [First edition 2004.]

To Read or Not to Read: A Question of National Consequences. Washington, DC: National Endowment for the Arts, 2007.

Reading on the Rise. Washington, DC: National Endowment for the Arts, 2009.

BOOKS ABOUT DANA GIOIA

Brennan, Matthew. *Dana Gioia: A Critical Introduction.* West Chester, PA: Story Line Press, 2012.

Foley, Jack, ed. *The "Fallen Western Star" Wars.* Oakland, CA: Scarlet Tanager Books, 2001.

Hagstrom, Jack W. C., and Bill Morgan, eds. *Dana Gioia: A Descriptive Bibliography with Critical Essays.* Jackson, MS: Parrish House, 2002.

Lindner, April. *Dana Gioia.* Western Writers Series 143. Boise: Boise State University, 2000. [Revised edition 2003.]

Peich, Michael. *Dana Gioia and Fine Press Printing: A Bibliographic Checklist*. New York: Kelly/Winterton Press, 2000.

FURTHER READING

Bauerlein, Mark, ed. *National Endowment for the Arts: A History (1965-2008)*. Washington, DC: National Endowment for the Arts, 2008.

McPhillips, Robert. *The New Formalism: A Critical Introduction*. Expanded ed. Cincinnati: Textos Books, 2005.

Schwartz, Carol A., ed. *Poetry Criticism: Criticism of the Works of the Most Significant and Widely Studied Poets of World Literature*. Vol. 226, Dana Gioia, 1-70. Farmington Hills, MI: Gale, 2020.

Walzer, Kevin. *The Ghost of Tradition: Expansive Poetry and Postmodernism*. Ashland, OR: Story Line Press, 1998.

Welford, Theresa Malphrus. *Transatlantic Connections: The Movement and New Formalism*. Pasadena, CA: Story Line Press, 2019.

SELECTED REFERENCE ARTICLES

Austenfeld, Thomas. "The Drama of Shaping a Lyrical Moment: An Approach to the Poetry of Dana Gioia." In *New Pilgrimages: Selected Papers from the IAUPE Beijing Conference in 2013*, 244-58. Beijing: Tsinghua University Press, 2015.

Balée, Susan. "Poems for Those Aching for Words." Review of *Interrogations at Noon*. *Philadelphia Inquirer*, April 15, 2001, H13-14.

Bauerlein, Mark. "The Gioia Effect." *First Things*, October 19, 2016.

Bilbro, Jeffrey. "Teaching Us the Names: The Poetry of Dana Gioia." Review of *99 Poems*. *Books and Culture*, October 7, 2016.

Clausen, Christopher. "Poetry Formal and Free." *Sewanee Review* 99.4 (1991): xcvii-c.

———. "Culture and the Subculture." *Commentary* 95.2 (1993): 75-76.

D'Evelyn, Thomas. "Poetry That Matters: A Plunge into Shared Experience." Review of *The Gods of Winter*. *Christian Science Monitor*, July 2 1991, 14.

Donaghy, Michael. "Dana Gioia—Criticism and Hedonism." In *The Shape of the Dance: Essays, Interviews and Digressions*, edited by Adam O'Riordan and Maddy Paxman, 74-78. London: Picador, 2009.

Doncu, Roxana Elena. "Coaxing Words into Form: The Poetry of Dana Gioia." In *Literary Form: Theories—Dynamics—Cultures, Perspectives on Literary Modelling*, edited by Robert Matthias Erdbeer et al. Heidelberg: Heidelberg University Press, 2018.

Foley, Jack. "The Achievement of Dana Gioia." In *The Dancer and the Dance: A Book of Distinctions, Poetry in the New Century*, 150-56. Los Angeles: Red Hen Press, 2008.

Hix, H. L. "Dana Gioia's Criticism." In *A Descriptive Bibliography with Critical Essays*, edited by Jack W. C. Hagstrom and Bill Morgan, 283-96. Jackson, MS: Parrish House, 2002.

Hren, Joshua, "Climbing to God on 'The Burning Ladder': Dana Gioia's *Via Negativa*." *Religion and the Arts* 23.1-2 (2019): 124-41.

Juster, A. M. "The Case for Dana Gioia." *CRB Digital*, May 15, 2016.

Kirsch, Adam. "The Poetry Problem: Can Poetry Matter?" *New York Sun*, September 18, 2002, 1,10.

Kramer, Hilton. "Poetry and the Silencing of Art." *New Criterion* (Feb. 1993): 4-9.

Lind, Michael. "Dana Gioia as a Literary Figure." In *A Descriptive Bibliography with Critical Essays*, edited by Jack W. C. Hagstrom and Bill Morgan, 297-300. Jackson, MS: Parrish House, 2002.

Maio, Samuel. "Dana Gioia's Dramatic Monologues." *The Formalist* 13.1 (2002): 63-72.

Mason, David, "Dana Gioia's Case for Poetry." *Sparrow* 60 (1993): 22-28.

———. "Dana Gioia." In *Encyclopedia of American Poetry: The Twentieth Century*, edited by Eric L. Haralson, 247-48. Chicago: Fitzroy Dearborn, 2001.

———. "The Inner Exile of Dana Gioia." *Sewanee Review* 123.1 (2015): 133-46.

Massimilla, Stephen. "The Achievement of Dana Gioia." Review of *99 Poems*. *Italian Americana* 35.1 (2017): 75-79.

Mattix, Micah. "Dana Gioia's Poetry." Review of *99 Poems*. *Washington Free Beacon*, March 19, 2016.

McCann, Janet. "Dana Gioia: A Contemporary Metaphysics." *Renascence* 61.3 (2009): 193-205.

McDowell, Robert. "The New Narrative Poetry." *Crosscurrents* 8.2 (1989) 30-38.

McPhillips, Robert. "Dana Gioia." In *The Oxford Companion to Twentieth-Century Poetry in English*, edited by Ian Hamilton, 188. New York: Oxford University Press, 1994.

Meyer, Bruce. "(Michael) Dana Gioia." In *Dictionary of Literary Biography: New Formalist Poets*. Vol. 282, edited by Jonathan N. Barron and Bruce Meyer. Detroit: Gale, 2003.

Middleton, David. "The Mystery of Things." Review of *99 Poems*. *Chronicles* (April 2017): 22-23.

Oxley, William. "(Michael) Dana Gioia." In *Contemporary Poets*. 6th ed., edited by Thomas Riggs, 388-89. Detroit: St. James Press, 1996.

——. "The First Shall Be Last." Review of *Interrogations at Noon*. *Acumen* 41 (2001): 101-4.

Perloff, Marjorie. "Poetry Doesn't Matter." *American Book Review* (Dec. 1993–Jan. 1994): 3, 5, 7, 9.

Russell, Peter. "Dana Gioia and the New Formalism." *Edge City Review* 1.2 (1994): 13-19.

Simpson, Louis. "On the Neglect of Poetry in the United States." *New Criterion* (Sep. 1991): 81-85.

Stevenson, Anne. "The Poetry of Dana Gioia: A Review of *The Gods of Winter*." In *Between the Iceberg and the Ship: Selected Essays*, 156-58. Ann Arbor: University of Michigan Press, 1998.

Thwaite, Anthony. "Preface." In *Contemporary Poets*. 6th ed., edited by Thomas Riggs, vii–viii. Detroit: St. James Press, 1996.

Turco, Lewis. "(Michael) Dana Gioia." In *Dictionary of Literary Biography: American Poets Since World War II: Third Series*. Vol. 120, edited by R. S. Gwynn, 84-90. Detroit: Gale Research, 1992.

Wilson, James Matthew. *The Catholic Imagination in Modern American Poetry*. Milwaukee: Wiseblood Books, 2014.

——. "The World of New Formalism." In *The Fortunes of Poetry in an Age of Unmaking*, 77-99. Oregon: Wiseblood Books, 2015.

Winchell, Mark Royden. "Dana Gioia." In *Oxford Encyclopedia of American Literature.* Vol. 2, edited by Jay Parini, 115-17. New York: Oxford University Press, 2004.

Young, R. V. "The Place of Poetry in Twitterland." *Modern Age* 55.3 (2013): 49-56.

INDEX